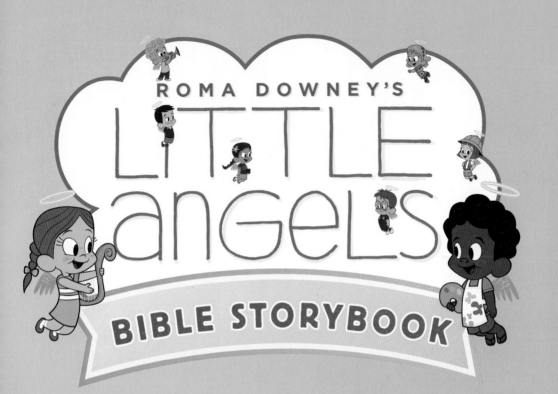

ROMA DOWNEY'S LITTLE ANGELS

BIBLE STORYBOOK

TYNDALE HOUSE PUBLISHERS, INC. CAROL STREAM, ILLINOIS

ROMA DOWNEY'S
LITTLE ANGELS

BIBLE STORYBOOK

WITH CAROLYN LARSEN

Visit Tyndale online at www.tyndale.com.

To learn more about the Little Angels, visit www.littleangels.com.

TYNDALE is a registered trademark of Tyndale House Publishers, Inc.

The Tyndale Kids logo is a trademark of Tyndale House Publishers, Inc.

Little Angels Bible Storybook

Bible character illustrations by Rick Incrocci

Stories by Carolyn Larsen

Cover designed by Jennifer Ghionzoli

Interior designed by Jennifer Ghionzoli and Educational Publishing Concepts

Edited by Brittany Buczynski

For manufacturing information regarding this product, please call 1-800-323-9400.

Library of Congress Cataloging-in-Publication Data
Larsen, Carolyn, date.
  Little angels Bible storybook / Carolyn Larsen ; illustrated by Rick Incrocci.
    p. cm. — (Roma Downey's little angels series)
  ISBN 978-1-4143-7022-4
1. Bible stories, English.   I. Incrocci, Rick.   II. Title.
  BS551.3.L368 2012
  220.9'505—dc23   2012012849

Printed in China

18	17	16	15	14	13	12
7	6	5	4	3	2	1

_____

Presented to

_____

by

_____

on

Table of Contents

STORIES FROM THE OLD TESTAMENT

STORIES FROM THE NEW TESTAMENT

Dear Parents, Grandparents, and Teachers,

I am so glad you have chosen to share this *Little Angels Bible Storybook* with your children! The Little Angels project is near and dear to my heart, and I am so eager to share it with you.

> *God in heaven, my Savior dear,*
> *Watch over my children and draw thou near.*
> *Send your little angels to be at their side*
> *To light and to guard, to love and to guide.*

This sweet nighttime prayer from my own childhood was one of the inspirations for the little angels brand. As you may know, I played an angel on television for almost 10 years, bringing a message of God's love to millions of people around the world. And now I want to bring the same message to your kids.

In Little Angels, four-year-old twins Alex and Zoe have eight little angels looking out for them. The angels live on a mural on the nursery's ceiling and come to life when the kids need them most. They act as teachers, protectors, and friends—to instruct and guide. Each angel has a distinct personality, and I know your kids will just love every one of them!

This Bible storybook will provide your children with wonderful retellings of 100 best-loved Bible stories. In addition to the Bible stories, children will learn practical skills such as their ABCs, colors, and numbers. It will also teach them core family values, such as the importance of being kind and sharing, of being truthful and honest, and of showing gratitude and love.

Alex and Zoe face the same challenges all kids do, and our Little Angels are always there to help them along the way. And because the angels are messengers from God, our Little Angels are there to remind Alex and Zoe that they are never alone, for God is always watching over them and loving them.

May God bless you always, and I pray that you will enjoy reading these Bible stories with your little ones.

Love,
Roma

Meet Alex, Zoe, and the Little Angels!

Alex and *Zoe* are twins. They love to learn and laugh. God loves them very much. He loves you, too!

Uriel, also known as Uri, is the Angel of Creativity. He loves to paint and create wonderful things.

Charmeine, also known as Charmy, is the Angel of Harmony. She carries a harp and sings. She helps everyone be kind and get along.

Hamaliel, also known as Hammy, is the Angel of Logic. He's great at solving problems and mysteries.

Dina is the Angel of Learning. She loves to help you think and learn how to do things.

Michael is the Archangel. He is the leader of our angel friends.

Ariel is the Guardian Angel. She keeps Alex and Zoe safe and helps them stay out of trouble.

Hayley is the Animal Facts Angel. She knows all about animals. She teaches us about God's creatures and how we should be kind to them.

Gabriel is the Messenger Angel. He carries a trumpet and tells us important things.

OLD
TESTAMENT

God Makes Wonderful Things

GENESIS 1:1—2:3

What was the world like before
God started making things?
There was nothing! Before
God created things
there was no earth.
There was no sky. There
were no oceans.
There were no
plants, no animals,
and no people.
There was nothing.
Then God
said, "Let there
be light," and
creation began!

On Day One of creation, God made light and dark. He called them day and night. God liked what he made.

The next day, Day Two, God made the sky. He liked what he made. On Day Three, God made the land and the seas. He made all the plants that grow on the land. God liked everything he made.

God made the sun and moon and stars

I learned that . . .

God made all the colors! He used blue for the sky; green for grass; orange, pink, and blue for sunsets; and red, purple, and yellow for flowers. Sometimes God mixes colors to make new ones. Blue and yellow go together to make green. Red and yellow mixed together make orange. God made colors, colors everywhere!

21

on Day Four. He liked what he made then, too. On Day Five, God filled the seas with all kinds of fish. He made birds to fly through the sky. God liked all he made.

Day Six was the day he made all the animals that live on the land. He also made his greatest creation on Day Six. He made the very first people! God liked everything he made. He liked it all! So, on Day Seven, God rested.

I can ... Draw a picture, but choose strange colors for things. Use your imagination. How about pink grass and a green sky? What are your favorite colors?

· ·

Dear God,
Thank you for all the wonderful things you made! You thought of exciting and funny and pretty and really special things to make. Thank you most of all for making me! *Amen*

so I **PRAY** ...

· ·

*The heavens are yours,
and the earth is yours;
everything in the world is
yours—you created it all.*

PSALM 89:11

God Makes Adam and Eve

GENESIS 2:4-25

God made the earth, sky, and oceans. He made plants and animals and fish and birds too. The last thing God made was very special. He took some plain old dust from the ground and made a man from it. Then he breathed life into the man. He named the man Adam.

God made a beautiful garden for Adam to live in. It was called the Garden of Eden. God told Adam that he could eat fruit from any tree in the Garden except one. He could not eat fruit from the tree that grew in the middle of the Garden. It was called the Tree of the Knowledge of Good and Evil. God said Adam would die if he ate from that tree.

God saw that Adam was

I learned that . . .

God cares about my problems. He made a beautiful place for Adam to live. He gave Adam jobs to do. But God saw that Adam was lonely. He made Eve to be Adam's wife. God solved Adam's problem.

lonely. He needed a special friend. God brought all the animals to Adam so that he could give them names. None of the animals were the right friend for Adam. He was still lonely. So God made Adam fall asleep. While Adam was sleeping, God took out one of Adam's ribs. He used it to make the first woman. Her name was Eve. She became Adam's wife. They were very happy together!

I can ... Be a good friend! Help someone who is lonely like Adam was. What can you do to help this person feel better? Can you draw a picture? Can you go visit? Can you call the person on the phone?

. . . .

Dear God,
Thank you for giving Adam a friend when he was lonely. Thank you for caring when I feel sad or lonely. Thank you for loving me so much. Help me to be a good friend. *Amen*

so I PRAY...

. . . .

*Give all your worries
and cares to God,
for he cares about you.*

1 PETER 5:7

The First Sin

GENESIS 3

God gave Adam and Eve one rule. They could not eat fruit from the Tree of the Knowledge of Good and Evil that grew in the middle of the Garden.

One day a snake came to Eve and asked, "Did God really say you can't eat fruit from any tree that grows in the Garden?"

"No," Eve answered. "We just can't eat fruit from the tree in the middle of the Garden. If we eat that fruit, we will die."

"You won't die," the snake said. "God doesn't want you to eat that fruit because it will make

you as smart as he is."
This wasn't true. The snake was lying!

Instead of listening to God, Eve believed the snake's lie. Eve thought being as smart as God sounded good so she ate the fruit. She gave some to Adam, and he ate it too. Right away they knew they had broken the rule God gave them. So they hid from him.

"Adam, where are you?" God said.

I learned that . . .

God watches the things I do. He knows when I obey him and when I don't. Disobeying him leads to trouble. It makes God happy when I obey him and follow his rules.

"I'm hiding," Adam answered.

"Why?" God asked. "Did you eat the fruit that I told you not to eat?"

"Eve gave it to me. It's her fault," Adam said.

"No, it wasn't my fault. The snake tricked me!" Eve said.

God was sad that Adam and Eve had disobeyed him. "You have to leave the Garden," he told them. He put guards at the entrance to the Garden so Adam and Eve could never go back in!

I can... Stack some blocks one on top of the other. As your tower gets taller and taller, what finally happens? It tumbles, right? If the blocks are stacked too high, then the tower will fall. The things you do make other things happen.

. . . .

Dear God,
Sometimes I don't do what's right. I know that makes you sad. I'm sorry for making you sad. Help me to obey you and follow your rules. I love you. *Amen*

SO I PRAY...

. . . .

Be careful to obey all these commands I am giving you. Show love to the LORD your God by walking in his ways and holding tightly to him.

DEUTERONOMY 11:22

Noah Builds a Big Boat

GENESIS 6:1—7:10

The people on earth stopped following God. They didn't obey him. They didn't care about him at all. People were mean to each other. They cheated and lied. God was sad because of the way people acted. But he had a plan to make things better.

God asked Noah to help him.
Noah was the only man who still obeyed God.

"Noah," God said, "I'm going to send a big flood
that will cover everything on earth. All the people.
All the animals.
All the plants.
Everything. But
I want you to be
safe. So you must
build a big boat."
Noah was happy
to do what God
said. God told
Noah exactly how
to make the boat.
It was going to be
very big!

33

Then God told Noah to take two of every kind of animal on earth inside the boat. Noah and his family would go into the boat too. "Don't forget to bring food for the animals and your family," God said. They would be in the boat for a long time. But they would be safe from the big flood because they followed God's plan.

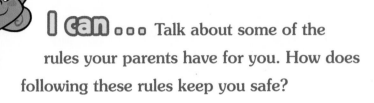

I can ... Talk about some of the rules your parents have for you. How does following these rules keep you safe?

· ·

Dear God,
Thank you for having a plan to keep me safe. Help me to obey your plan and do what you want me to do.
Amen

· ·

"I know the plans I have for you," says the LORD. "They are plans for good and not for disaster, to give you a future and a hope."

JEREMIAH 29:11

God Sends a Big Flood

GENESIS 7:11 — 9:19

God told Noah that a big flood was coming.
He wanted Noah to be safe so
he told Noah to build
a big boat. Noah
and his family
and two of
every kind
of animal
on earth
went inside
the boat.
As
soon as
God
closed

the door of the big boat, it started to rain outside. It rained and rained and rained. It rained for 40 days and 40 nights without stopping! Before long the water flooded the earth. But Noah and his family and all the animals inside the big boat were safe. After a while, everything on earth was underwater. God remembered Noah and his family in the big boat. He told

I learned that . . .

God makes promises to his people. If I will trust his promises, I can be at peace. I can know that he is taking care of things. God will never break his promises. I can always trust him!

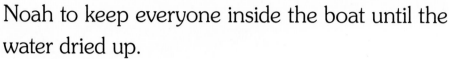

Noah to keep everyone inside the boat until the water dried up.

Noah and his family were in the boat about a year before it was safe for them to come out. All the animals came out then too! The first thing Noah did was thank God for keeping them safe. Then God put a beautiful rainbow in the sky. "I will never again destroy the whole earth with a flood," God told Noah. "Every time you see a rainbow, it will remind you of this promise."

I can... Count by twos: "2 . . . 4 . . . 6 . . . 8 . . ." How far can you go counting by twos? God sent two of each kind of animal into the big boat.

- -

Dear God,
Thank you for your promise to never flood the whole earth again. Thank you for all your promises to love me, teach me, and protect me. *Amen*

so I PRAY...

- -

*God's way is perfect.
All the LORD's promises
prove true. He is a shield
for all who look to
him for protection.*

PSALM 18:30

The Tower of Babel

GENESIS 11:1-9

For a while after the big flood, things on earth were okay. Everyone got along. That was easy because everyone on earth spoke the same language. Then a few men had an idea. "Let's make a new building," they said.

"That's a great idea," someone said. "And we don't have to stop with just one building. Let's build a whole city!"

Another man had an even bigger idea. "Let's make one of the buildings in the city a very tall tower. It will be so tall that everyone in the world will know about it. We will become famous for building such a tall tower!"

The people agreed. "We will be powerful! Then no other nations will attack us. We will be able to stay together forever!" the crowd shouted.

God saw the city the people were building. He saw the very

I learned that . . .

God has the power to do anything. He wants people to depend on his power and trust him to take care of them.

tall tower. He heard the things they were saying.
God was not happy about any of it. "These people
think that nothing is impossible for them," he said.
"I must stop them. I will make the people all speak
different languages. Then they will not be able
to work together. They will not think they are so
strong then."

So that's what God did. The people were
confused and could not understand each other.
Everyone scattered! Different groups moved all
over the world so they could be with people who
spoke the same language they did. The city where
this happened is called Babel because that is
where God mixed up the languages.

I can ... Learn this little song: "My God is so big, so strong, and so mighty. There's nothing my God cannot do." Every time you sing it, remind yourself of God's power.

. . . .

Dear God,
Thank you for being so strong and powerful. Thank you for using your power to take care of me. *Amen*

. . . .

All the nations you made will come and bow before you, Lord; they will praise your holy name.

PSALM 86:9

Abraham Moves to a New Land

GENESIS 11:26—12:9

Abraham and his wife, Sarah, lived in Abraham's hometown near his father and brothers. One day Abraham's father decided to take his whole family

and move away. They were going to a land called Canaan. It was a long journey. They walked for a long time. Finally they stopped in a little town and decided to live there instead. They didn't ever make it to Canaan.

A few years later Abraham's father died. God had said to Abraham, "Pack up everything you own and all your family. I want you to move to a new place. I will show you where to go." Abraham obeyed

I learned that...

When God has a job for his people to do, he calls them to do it. His people need to trust him and follow what he tells them to do—even if they can't see where they are going. Trusting God is best!

God. He didn't know where God was leading him, but he took his wife, Sarah, and his nephew, Lot. He took all his animals and everything he owned. He took all the people who worked for him too.

God led him to the land of Canaan. When Abraham got there, God came to him and said, "I will give this land to your family and to all your grandchildren and great-grandchildren." Abraham was so happy! He thanked God and worshiped him.

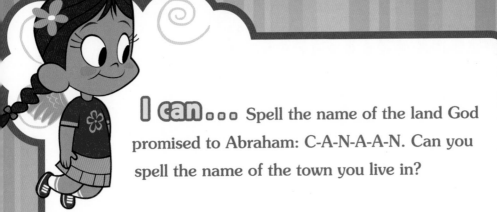

I can... Spell the name of the land God promised to Abraham: C-A-N-A-A-N. Can you spell the name of the town you live in?

. . . .

Dear God,
Thank you that I can always trust you. You know the future. So even when I don't understand why things happen, I will trust you! *Amen*

so I **PRAY...**

. . . .

Trust in the LORD with all your heart; do not depend on your own understanding.

PROVERBS 3:5

Abraham and Lot Go Different Ways

GENESIS 13:1-13

Abraham was traveling to find food and water for his animals. He took his wife, Sarah, and his nephew, Lot, with him. Abraham was very rich. He had lots of animals and servants and lots of silver and gold to pack up and bring on the trip. Lot was also very rich. His servants and animals were traveling with them too.

When they stopped to camp, they realized that they had a problem. The place where they camped didn't have enough food and water for all of their animals. Soon fights broke out between Abraham's servants and Lot's servants. They all fought to get food and water for the animals.

Finally the fighting got so bad that Abraham went to Lot and said, "This fighting needs to stop. We are family so we shouldn't be

fighting. There is plenty of land around us. You choose the land you want. If you want to live over here on the right, then I'll move to the left. If you want the land on the left, then I will move to the right. Just choose where you want to live."

Lot looked around. On one side was good land with lots of water and grass for the animals. That's the land Lot chose. So Abraham took his family, servants, and animals and moved to the other land, called Canaan.

I can ... Share what you have with others! It's not easy to share sometimes, but God tells you to do it. What do you have that you can share?

Dear God,
I know that it is important to share with others. Help me to be kind and generous. Help me to never be selfish. Amen

SO I PRAY...

John replied, "If you have two shirts, give one to the poor. If you have food, share it with those who are hungry."

LUKE 3:11

God Makes a Promise to Abraham

GENESIS 17

When Abraham was 99 years old, God came to him and said, "If you will obey me, I will make a great promise to you. I promise that I will give you a big, big family! I will make you the father of many

nations. Your family will be big and
powerful. There will be kings in your family!
My promise to you will last forever. I will always
be your God and the
God of all your
grandchildren
and great-
grandchildren.
I also promise
to give the land
of Canaan, where
you live now,
to you and your
family."
    Then God
made an even
more wonderful

I learned that . . .

God always keeps his
promises. Even when
it takes a long time,
we should keep
trusting God.
He does what he
says he will do . . .
always!

promise to Abraham and Sarah. He promised to give them a son! They had always wanted to have children. This boy would be the beginning of God's promise to give Abraham a big family. When Abraham heard this promise, he laughed to himself. He thought that he and Sarah were too old to have a baby! But God said, "No, you will have a son next year. I promise."

I can... Ask your mom or dad to help you make a list of some of God's promises to you.

. . . .

Dear God,
Thank you for your wonderful promises! I am so thankful that I can trust every one of them! *Amen*

so I PRAY...

. . . .

The Spirit is God's guarantee that he will give us the inheritance he promised and that he has purchased us to be his own people. He did this so we would praise and glorify him.

EPHESIANS 1:14

Angels Visit Abraham

GENESIS 18:1-16

One hot day Abraham was sitting by the door of his tent when he saw three men standing nearby. He didn't know them, but he invited them to come and sit in the cool shade.

"Let me get some water for you, and I will have Sarah cook you some food," Abraham said. While the men were eating, they asked Abraham where Sarah was. Abraham told them that she was inside the tent.

One of the men said, "I will come back this way about this same time next year. By then Sarah will have a baby." Sarah was listening from inside the tent. It was funny to think of her

I learned that . . .

God knows everything that is going to happen in the future. He wants me to trust him to do the things he promises. Nothing is hidden from God, and nothing is impossible for God to do.

old, worn-out body having a baby. And how could Abraham, who was even older, become a father? The whole idea made her laugh. She giggled silently. She and Abraham had wanted to have a baby for a long time, but now they were both too old. "Why did Sarah laugh?" the Lord asked. "Is anything too hard for God?"

"I didn't laugh," Sarah said. She was afraid that she had made God angry.

"I heard you laugh," the Lord said. Then the men got up and left.

I can... Draw a picture of something God made that looks impossible. Maybe it's a huge bird that can fly or a kangaroo that keeps her baby in a pouch. What do you think is God's most amazing creation?

. . . .

Dear God,
I can't hide my thoughts from you. Thank you that you see my heart and know that I want to serve you. Thank you for knowing what my future holds. *Amen*

. . . .

You love him even though you have never seen him. Though you do not see him now, you trust him; and you rejoice with a glorious, inexpressible joy.

1 PETER 1:8

Isaac Is Born

GENESIS 21:1-7

For a very long time Abraham and Sarah had wanted to have a baby. God had promised them that they would have a big family. But now they were very old and had no children.

They waited and waited. How could they have a big family if they didn't have any children? Would God keep his promise?

He did! Sarah gave birth to a baby boy. God's plan was perfect. He knew when it was the right time for Sarah to have her baby. Everything happened just like God said it would.

Sarah and Abraham were thrilled to see that God kept his promise.

I learned that ...

Even if it takes a very long time, God will keep his promises. I can always trust him to do what he says. God knows the best time for everything.

They were so happy to finally have a child! They named their little boy Isaac. The name Isaac means "laughter." God's promise for Abraham's big family was coming true!

I can... Sing a happy birthday song for Isaac! Birthdays are great days to celebrate God's gift of life and family. When is your birthday?

Dear God,
Thank you for always keeping your promises. Thank you that I can trust what you say, even if it seems to be taking a long time. I know you will do what you promised. *Amen*

so I **PRAY...**

Let us hold tightly without wavering to the hope we affirm, for God can be trusted to keep his promise.

HEBREWS 10:23

A Bride for Isaac

GENESIS 24

Abraham was very old now. There was one thing
that he wanted before he died. He wanted his son,
Isaac, to marry a girl from their home country.
So Abraham told his best servant to go back to

their homeland and find a bride for Isaac. This was a big, important job. The servant loaded 10 camels with expensive gifts and traveled to the faraway land.

When he arrived, the servant wasn't sure how to know which girl would be the right bride for Isaac. So he prayed. "God, I'm standing here by a well where the people of this town come to get water to drink.

I will ask one of the girls for a drink of water.
If she gives me water, and offers to get water for
my camels, too, then I will know she is the right
girl for Isaac."

As soon as the servant had finished praying,
a beautiful girl came to the
well. The servant asked
her for a drink of water.
She answered, "Of
course. I'll get you a
drink, and then
let me get
water for your
camels, also."
The servant told
her about Isaac.
The beautiful girl,
named Rebekah,
agreed to go
with the servant
and marry
Isaac.

I can ... Put a towel or a small pillow under the back of your shirt and pretend you're a camel! Do you know why camels have humps on their backs? The humps store fat and water so that camels can go on very long trips without stopping to eat or drink. Camels with one hump live in the desert and can walk a long way without having water.

. . . .

Dear God,
Please guide me. Show me what you want me to do for you. Guide me in how to live my life for you. *Amen*

so I PRAY...

. . . .

**Seek his will in all you do,
and he will show you
which path to take.**

PROVERBS 3:6

67

Esau and Jacob Are Born

GENESIS 25:19-26

Rebekah was brought from Abraham's homeland to marry his son, Isaac. They were very happy together except for one thing. Rebekah was not able to have children, and they wanted

very badly to have a family. Isaac knew what to do. He begged God to let them have a baby. God heard Isaac's prayer, and he answered it in an amazing way!

Soon Rebekah was going to have not just one baby. She was going to have twins! But the babies inside her seemed to fight with each other. She didn't understand why this was happening. So she asked God

I learned that . . .

Even before babies are born, God has a plan for their lives. Every person matters because God made each of us and loves us. We are all special to God.

what was going on with her two children. "Each of these two boys you are having will one day be in charge of a powerful nation. The two countries will be enemies. The nation led by your older son will serve the nation led by your younger son," God said.

When the babies were born, they were two boys, just as God had said they would be. The boy born first had very hairy skin. He was named Esau. The second boy was born holding on to his brother's heel. He was named Jacob.

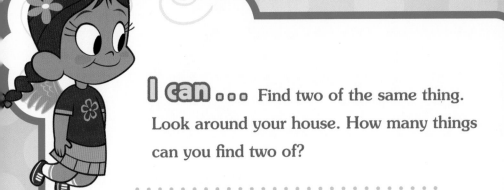

I can . . . Find two of the same thing. Look around your house. How many things can you find two of?

. . . .

Dear God,
It's kind of amazing to think that you had a plan for me before I was even born. It makes me happy that you know me so well! Help me to follow your plan. *Amen*

. . . .

You saw me before I was born. Every day of my life was recorded in your book. Every moment was laid out before a single day had passed.

PSALM 139:16

Esau Sells His Birthright

GENESIS 25:27-34

Isaac and Rebekah's twin boys, Esau and Jacob, grew up. Esau became a hunter. He liked to be outside hunting food for the family to eat. Jacob liked to stay at home and help his mother with things.

One day Esau came home from

a hunting trip. He was tired and hungry. Jacob was cooking some stew when Esau got home. "I'm starving. Can I have some of that stew?" Esau asked.

Jacob saw a chance to get something he wanted. "Sure, you can have some stew," Jacob said. "But only if you give me the family birthright." Esau owned the birthright because it was given to

I learned that . . .

We should always show respect for things that are important. God wants me to take good care of everything he has given me. Even when I'm tired or hungry, I still need to be respectful and make wise decisions.

the oldest son in a family. The son who owned the birthright would be the leader of the family one day.

The birthright was a very important thing. But Esau was so hungry, and he made a very bad decision. "What good is it to have the birthright if I starve to death?" Esau said. "Just give me some stew. You can have the birthright." So Esau traded the honor of having the family birthright for a bowl of stew.

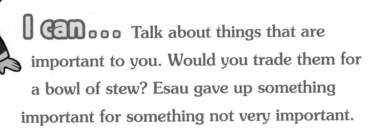

I can... Talk about things that are important to you. Would you trade them for a bowl of stew? Esau gave up something important for something not very important.

. . . .

Dear God,
Thank you for this reminder to take care of what's important. Help me to make good choices and respect the things you give me. *Amen*

. . . .

Seek the Kingdom of God above all else, and live righteously, and he will give you everything you need.

MATTHEW 6:33

Jacob Tricks His Father

GENESIS 27:1—28:9

Isaac was old and sick. He knew he would die soon. He called for his oldest son, Esau, to come to him. "Bring me my favorite dinner. After I eat, I will give you my blessing," Isaac said. The blessing meant that Esau would be in charge of the whole family. He would be the new family leader.

Esau left right away to hunt meat for the dinner. His mother, Rebekah, heard what Isaac said. She wanted her other son, Jacob, to get the blessing instead of Esau. So while Esau was gone, she cooked dinner. She told Jacob to dress in Esau's clothes so he would smell like Esau. Isaac was almost blind. He couldn't see much.

Jacob took the dinner to his father.

I learned that . . .

God wants us to treat each other fairly and tell the truth to each other. That means we should never steal or cheat or lie. We should always try to be kind and loving.

"Eat your dinner, Father. Then give me your blessing," Jacob said.

"Are you Esau?" Isaac asked. "You sound like Jacob, but you smell like Esau."

"Yes, I am Esau," Jacob lied. So Isaac gave the blessing to Jacob.

When Esau came home and found out what had happened, he was very angry. Jacob was afraid that Esau might hurt him, so he left home and went to live in another land.

I can... Make up a happy song to sing that will show others how much you love them. How else can you be nice to others?

. . . .

Dear God,
Jacob wasn't very nice to his brother. Help me to always be kind to others, especially to my family. *Amen*

SO I PRAY...

. . . .

Do to others whatever you would like them to do to you.

MATTHEW 7:12

Joseph's Coat of Many Colors

GENESIS 37:1-11

Jacob moved away from home because his brother, Esau, was very angry with him. He was afraid his brother would hurt him. Jacob traveled for a while and finally settled in Canaan.

Jacob got married and had 12 sons. One son, named Joseph, was his favorite son. Joseph and his

brothers took care of his father's flocks of sheep. When Joseph went home, he told his father about the bad things his brothers did. This got his brothers in trouble. Joseph's brothers were angry with him for that. They were also jealous of the special way their father treated Joseph. He gave Joseph a fancy coat of many colors. It was nicer than any of their coats.

One day

I learned that . . .

God has many ways of speaking to his people. For Joseph, God showed him things through his dreams. Dreams can just be dreams, or they can be messages from God. We can also hear God's messages by praying and reading the Bible.

Joseph told his brothers about a dream he had. He dreamed that they were all out in the field tying up bundles of grain. All their grain bundles bowed down to his. Then he had another dream that the sun, moon, and stars bowed down to him. When Joseph told his brothers and his father about that dream, none of them were happy. They didn't think they would bow down to Joseph someday.

I can... Draw Joseph wearing his coat of many colors. Do you think it had stripes, like a rainbow? Do you think it had colorful shapes, like purple triangles or green squares? Use lots of different colors in your picture!

Dear God,
Thank you for all the ways you speak to your children. Help me to always know when you are speaking to me.
Amen

[Jesus said,] "I am the good shepherd; I know my own sheep, and they know me."

JOHN 10:14

Joseph's Brothers Sell Him

GENESIS 37:18-35

Joseph's brothers did not like him. He told their father about the bad things they did. Joseph was their father's favorite son. He got special gifts from their father like a fancy, colorful coat. Joseph had dreams about all of his family bowing down to him.

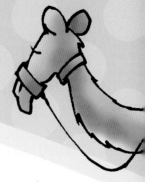

One day the brothers were watching their father's sheep out in a field when they saw Joseph coming. "Here comes the dreamer," they said. "Let's get rid of him," one brother said.

"Wait a minute," another one said. "There's an empty well over here. Let's just throw him in there and forget about him."

The brothers agreed. So they took off Joseph's fancy coat and threw him in the

I learned that...

When bad things happen, it doesn't mean God has stopped taking care of us. Bad things happened to Joseph, but God used those things for good one day.

deep hole in the ground. They were going to leave him there.

The brothers were eating dinner later when they saw some travelers coming. The men were traders going to Egypt. Joseph's brothers sold him to the traders so they would take Joseph to Egypt and sell him to be a slave. Then the brothers went home and told their father that his favorite son was gone.

I can ... Make a sound like a sheep—"baa-baa." Joseph's brothers were watching sheep for their father. Did you know that sheep have very good hearing, but they can't see things right behind them? That's why sheep need a shepherd to keep them safe.

Dear God,
Thank you for using bad things for good. I know you will guide and protect me, just like you did for Joseph. *Amen*

so I PRAY...

We can rejoice, too, when we run into problems and trials, for we know that they help us develop endurance.

ROMANS 5:3

God Helps Joseph

GENESIS 39:1—42:5

Joseph was sold to be a slave in Egypt. But he was good at his work, and things were going well for Joseph—until someone lied about him. Then he was put in prison. Joseph didn't understand why all this was happening, but he never stopped trusting God.

One night Pharaoh, the ruler of Egypt, had dreams he could not understand. None of his advisers could explain them. Pharaoh heard that a prisoner named Joseph could explain dreams, so he brought him to his palace. God helped Joseph explain that the dreams were a warning. Egypt would have seven good years of crops and then seven years of no crops at all! Pharaoh was so happy to have

I learned that . . .

Even when bad things happen, God is still working. If I keep trusting him, he will help me through all my problems.

his dreams explained that he took Joseph out of prison! He made Joseph the ruler of Egypt, second only to Pharaoh himself.

Joseph worked hard to store grain during the seven good years so that Egypt would have food during the seven bad years. Countries around Egypt ran out of food, and people came from all over to ask Joseph for help. One day, Joseph's brothers came to Egypt to get food. They didn't know they would be talking to the brother they had sold into slavery.

I can... Talk about a rule you have to follow to stay safe. Rules are good because they protect us from getting hurt. Can you think of a rule that would be easy to follow—like "No eating worms"? Write your rule on a sign.

Dear God,
Thank you for the story of Joseph. Help me to always trust you even when life gets hard, just like he did!
Amen

so I PRAY...

The Lord is a shelter for the oppressed, a refuge in times of trouble.

PSALM 9:9

Joseph Has a Secret

GENESIS 45:1-15

Pharaoh made Joseph the ruler of Egypt. Joseph
stored lots of grain so that the people of Egypt
would have enough food during seven years when
no crops would grow. The countries around Egypt
had a famine too. Many people came from far

away to ask Joseph for food. Joseph had ended up in Egypt because his own brothers sold him into slavery. They didn't know what happened to him after he got to Egypt.

But one day, Joseph's brothers came to Egypt to see if they could get food for their families. The brothers didn't recognize Joseph when they spoke with him. But Joseph knew them. All his life, Joseph trusted

I learned that...

Forgiveness is the best way. Joseph had a lot of reasons to want to get even with his brothers. But he knew that forgiving them was better because forgiveness is God's way.

God. Because he served God, Joseph decided to forgive. When he saw his brothers, he did not try to get even with them for wanting to hurt him. Instead, he was happy to see them and gave them plenty of food.

Joseph finally told his brothers who he was. He said, "Don't be afraid. I know you tried to hurt me, but God used it for good! I can save your families and our father now because God put me in charge here. Go get our father and bring him to Egypt. I will take care of all of you!"

I can... Forgive someone who was mean to you or hurt your feelings. God wants us to always forgive others and ask forgiveness when we do wrong things. Do you need to ask someone to forgive something you did?

Dear God,

Help me to be as forgiving as Joseph was. When someone hurts me, remind me that getting even will not make me feel better. Help me to be loving, like you are. *Amen*

so I PRAY...

Even if that person wrongs you seven times a day and each time turns again and asks forgiveness, you must forgive.

LUKE 17:4

Hebrew Slaves Work in Egypt

EXODUS 1

Many years after Joseph lived in Egypt, a bad thing happened to the Hebrew people. A new king began ruling in Egypt. He didn't remember anything about Joseph. He even forgot how Joseph saved the Egyptians from being hungry during the famine.

This king didn't like that there were so many Hebrew people in his country. He was afraid the Hebrews would try to rule Egypt. So he decided to make the Hebrew people his slaves. He gave them a very hard job to do. They had to make bricks using just mud and straw.

It was hard work. The king wanted to keep the Hebrews very busy. So he forced them to make more and more bricks.

The Hebrews were tired and sad because the Egyptians were so mean to them.

But God took care of his people. Many Hebrew babies were born. The Hebrew nation grew bigger and bigger. When the king heard about all the babies, he got more worried. Then he made a plan. The king ordered his people to throw all the Hebrew boy babies in the river. He didn't want those boys to grow up to be soldiers. Things were scary for the Hebrews. But God had a special plan for them.

I can ... Use your blocks to build a tall tower. Can you make it as tall as a building? Are your blocks as heavy as the bricks the Hebrews had to make?

· ·

Dear God,
Thank you for taking care of your people, the Hebrews. Thank you for taking care of me, too. I'm glad you always have a plan. *Amen*

SO I PRAY...

· ·

Only I can tell you the future before it even happens. Everything I plan will come to pass, for I do whatever I wish.

ISAIAH 46:10

God Takes Care of Baby Moses

EXODUS 2:1-10

The king of Egypt ordered that all the Hebrew boy babies had to be thrown in the river. One Hebrew woman had a baby boy. She loved him very much. She just couldn't let her boy get thrown in the river. So she hid him for three months.

When he grew bigger, it was hard to hide

him. So the woman made a basket from grass. She covered it with tar so it would float. Then she put her baby boy in the basket and set the basket in the Nile River. She told her daughter to hide close to the basket and watch what happened to it.

Soon her daughter came back and said, "The princess of Egypt found the basket. Even though she knows the baby is a Hebrew, she wants to keep him as her son!

I learned that . . .

Sometimes God gives us ideas about things we should do. He works his plans through people. He knew the princess would find baby Moses in the basket. It was all part of God's plan.

The princess named him Moses. But she needs a Hebrew woman to take care of the baby. Come quick, Momma! You can take care of him!" So the woman got to take care of her own baby boy. When he was older, she took him to the palace to live with the princess.

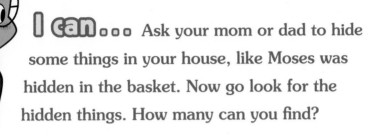

I can... Ask your mom or dad to hide some things in your house, like Moses was hidden in the basket. Now go look for the hidden things. How many can you find?

Dear God,
It is so amazing that we can be a part of your work. Thank you for using Moses' mother to save him. Thank you for using me, too! *Amen*

so I PRAY...

I am certain that God, who began the good work within you, will continue his work until it is finally finished on the day when Christ Jesus returns.

PHILIPPIANS 1:6

The Burning Bush

EXODUS 3:1—4:17

One day Moses saw a bush that was on fire.
It burned and burned but never burned up! He
went to look at it. When he got close, a voice
said, "Moses! Moses! You are on holy ground.

Take off your sandals." It was God—right there inside the burning bush.

God said, "I have seen that my people in Egypt are hurting. I have heard them crying because the Egyptians are mean to them. So I will save my people. Moses, I am sending you to the king of Egypt. Tell him to let my people go."

Moses was scared. "Why would the king listen to me?" he said.

God said, "I will be with you. Tell the people that I sent you."

"What if they don't believe me?" Moses asked.

God said, "Throw your shepherd's staff on the ground." A staff is a tall stick. When Moses threw his staff on the ground, it turned into a snake!

"Grab its tail," God said. Moses did, and the snake turned back into a shepherd's staff.

But Moses was still afraid to go talk to the king. He said, "I don't speak very well. Please send someone else."

God said, "Your brother, Aaron, can go with you. I will tell you what to say, and you tell Aaron. Then he can speak to the king." Finally Moses agreed to go.

I can ... Draw a picture of a burning bush. Color the fire bright red and yellow. When you mix red and yellow, what color do you get? Hang the picture on your wall. When you see it, remember that God always helps you do the work he wants you to do.

· ·

Dear God,
I'm glad that you help me when I'm scared. Thank you for listening and helping. *Amen*

· ·

I can do everything through Christ, who gives me strength.

PHILIPPIANS 4:13

Ten Terrible Troubles

EXODUS 7:14—12:36

Moses and Aaron went to the king of Egypt. They told him God wanted him to let the Hebrews leave Egypt. The king said no because he didn't want to lose his slaves. So God sent 10 terrible troubles, called "plagues." These bad things would show the king God's power.

The 10 plagues made life very hard for the Egyptians. But God protected the Hebrew people from these terrible troubles. After each one, Moses asked the king to let the people leave Egypt. The king always said no.

These were the 10 terrible troubles: First, God made all the water in Egypt turn to blood. Then, frogs covered everything. Next, God made little bugs fill the air. (They even got in peoples' mouths

I learned that...

God can do anything to make his plan happen. No one has more power than God. If we are following God, we don't have to be afraid. He will take care of us.

and eyes.) Flies everywhere were the next problem. Then, all the Egyptians cows and sheep died. After that, the Egyptians got sores all over their bodies. They hurt a lot. Then, God sent a storm that destroyed many plants. Next, God sent bugs that ate the rest of the plants. And then, God sent deep darkness to cover Egypt for three days. All these bad things came to Egypt. But God kept the Hebrew people safe.

The king had a very hard heart. He still would not let the people leave. Finally, God proved his power by making the oldest son in every Egyptian home die. This last thing made the king change his mind. He let Moses lead the Hebrew people out of Egypt.

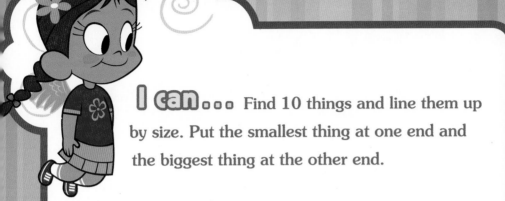

I can... Find 10 things and line them up by size. Put the smallest thing at one end and the biggest thing at the other end.

. . . .

Dear God,
I'm glad that I serve you. You are the most powerful! Amen

so **I PRAY...**

. . . .

Come and see what our God has done, what awesome miracles he performs for people!

PSALM 66:5

A Path through the Sea

EXODUS 14:1–15:21

Moses led the Hebrew people out of Egypt. God told Moses where to take them. They went as far as the Red Sea.

Back in Egypt, the king changed his mind. He wanted his slaves back. He took his army to chase

the Hebrews and bring them back to Egypt. When the Hebrews saw the army coming, they were scared. They said, "Moses, why did you take us out of Egypt? Now the king's whole army is coming, and they are going to hurt us!"

But Moses knew God was leading them and would protect them. God told Moses to hold his shepherd's staff out over the water of the Red Sea. The Egyptians

I learned that . . .

After God brought his people out of Egypt, he did not stop taking care of them. He saved them from the Egyptian army and kept them safe.

were getting closer. Then God made a strong wind blow. The wind parted the waters of the sea until there were two big walls of water with dry ground between them. Moses told the people to walk in the middle, between the walls of water. The Hebrews crossed the Red Sea on dry ground!

When the last Hebrew had crossed the sea, Moses put his staff down. Right away, the walls of water went back together. The Egyptian army rushed into the sea just as the water crashed down on them. God saved the Hebrew people!

I can . . . Take some pillows and put them together in a pile on the floor. Now pull them apart to make a path in the middle. Pretend the pillows are walls of water, just like in the Red Sea. Walk between them to make it to safety!

Dear God,
Thank you for finishing what you start. I'm glad that you are always in control. *Amen*

so I PRAY...

"I am the Alpha and the Omega—the beginning and the end," says the Lord God. "I am the one who is, who always was, and who is still to come—the Almighty One."

REVELATION 1:8

God Sends Special Food

EXODUS 16

About a month after the Hebrews left Egypt, the people started to get crabby. "We're hungry," they said. "Moses, why did you take us out of Egypt? At least we had food there. We are so hungry out here in the desert!"

God heard the people. He said, "Moses, I will send meat every night, and I will make bread fall down like rain every morning." God said that the people should pick up only what they needed to eat for each day. The food would rot if they took too much and tried to save it. But on the sixth day of the week, God told them to pick up enough food for two days. No food would come on the

I learned that . . .

God knows what I need. He cares about whether I have food to eat and water to drink. When we need something, we should pray to God and ask him for help.

seventh day because that was the Sabbath—a special day to rest and honor God.

That night hundreds of birds came to the camp. The people caught them and had meat for dinner. The next morning little white flakes covered the ground. It was food from heaven. They called it "manna," and it tasted sweet like honey. Some people disobeyed and tried to save extra food. It rotted, just as God said it would. On the sixth morning, there were twice as many flakes as usual. The people picked up twice what they needed and saved some for the next morning. It didn't go bad!

God sent new manna every morning, so the Hebrews always had enough to eat.

I can... Ask your mom or dad if you can help cook dinner. Can you cook some foods that are white, like manna? How about rice?

. . . .

Dear God,
Thank you for caring about my needs and giving me food to eat. I know some people don't have enough to eat. Please take care of them, too.
Amen

. . . .

I look up to the mountains—
does my help come from there?
My help comes from the LORD,
who made heaven and earth!

PSALM 121:1–2

Water from a Rock

EXODUS 17:1-7

God told the Hebrew people to keep walking.
He would lead them to their new land. They
walked in the desert and came to a place where
there was no water. The people were hot and
tired and thirsty. Soon they started to get crabby

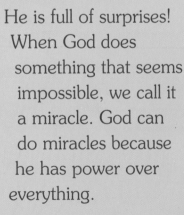

again. "Why did you take us out of Egypt?" they asked Moses. "We are so thirsty! How can we keep walking without anything to drink? Give us water!"

"Quiet!" said Moses. "Why are you yelling at me? Why don't you trust God?" But the people kept nagging and complaining. So Moses went to God and asked him what he should do about the people.

I learned that . . .

God can do things that no one else can do. He is full of surprises! When God does something that seems impossible, we call it a miracle. God can do miracles because he has power over everything.

God said, "Take your shepherd's staff and walk ahead of the people. Take some of the leaders with you. I will meet you at the rock by the big mountain over there. Hit the rock with your staff. Water will come flowing out for the people to drink. They will get as much water as they want." Moses did what God told him to do. Water came out of the rock! Soon the people had plenty of water to drink.

I can... Sing the song "Deep and Wide." It reminds us about the fountain of God's love flowing over us.

· · · · · · · · · · · · · · · · · · · ·

Dear God,
We can never guess what amazing things you might do to take care of us. Thank you for holy surprises!
Amen

· · · · · · · · · · · · · · · · · · · ·

Give thanks to the LORD, for he is good! His faithful love endures forever.

1 CHRONICLES 16:34

God's 10 Commandments

EXODUS 20:1-21

God called Moses to come
up to the top of a big
mountain called Mount
Sinai. God wanted to
give the people rules
for how they should
live. He told Moses the
rules, and then Moses
told the people.
God's rules would
help the people get
along and be nice to
each other. If the people
would follow these rules,
God would be pleased.
Ten of God's rules

taught the people how to treat each
other and how to treat God.

These rules are called the 10 Commandments:

1. Do not worship any other god . . . only the
   one true God.

2. Do not make
   anything to
   honor or pray
   to. Only honor
   and pray to God.

3. Do not use
   God's name
   in a bad way.

4. Always
   remember
   God's special
   day each week.

I learned that . . .

God's rules are good
for us. Following God's
rules will help me
to please him
and get along with
others. God gives us
rules to keep us safe
and to help us make
good choices.

5. Love your father and mother and show them respect.
6. Do not kill anyone.
7. If you get married, be a good husband or wife.
8. Do not steal or take things that are not yours.
9. Do not lie about others.
10. Do not want what belongs to someone else.

When God finished talking to Moses, the people saw thunder and lightning on the mountain top. The people were afraid. They didn't want God to talk to them. They wanted God to send all his messages through Moses!

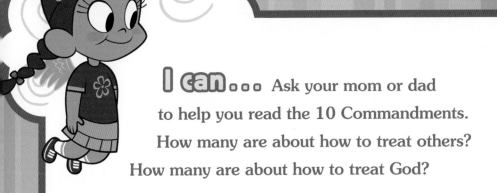

I can... Ask your mom or dad to help you read the **10 Commandments**. How many are about how to treat others? How many are about how to treat God?

. . . .

Dear God,
Following your rules isn't always easy. But I want to do what you say. Help me to trust you. *Amen*

. . . .

Obey me, and I will be your God, and you will be my people. Do everything as I say, and all will be well!

JEREMIAH 7:23

The Golden Calf

EXODUS 32

Moses was still up on the mountain getting commands from God for the people. He had been gone a long time. The people thought that he might not come back. So the people went to Aaron and said, "Make us some gods who can lead us. We need a leader, and we don't think Moses is ever coming back."

Aaron told the people to bring him all their gold rings and other gold jewelry. He melted the gold and shaped it to look like a baby cow, called a calf. The people were very happy and excited because it looked like the gods the Egyptians had. The people had a big party to honor the golden calf. There was singing and dancing and eating and drinking.

I learned that . . .

I can't honor something else and honor God. He is the only one I should honor and pray to!

But when God saw their party, he was not happy. "These people have hard hearts. They did not follow the rules I gave them," God said. He told Moses to go down and stop the people from honoring the golden calf.

Moses was very angry with the people. He melted the golden calf in a fire. When the gold dried, he pounded it into dust, mixed it with water, and made the people drink it. He reminded the people that they should pray only to God and honor only him.

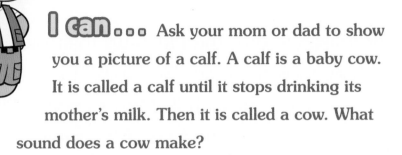

I can... Ask your mom or dad to show you a picture of a calf. A calf is a baby cow. It is called a calf until it stops drinking its mother's milk. Then it is called a cow. What sound does a cow make?

Dear God,
Thank you for hearing my prayers.
Help me to honor only you. *Amen*

SO I PRAY...

I, the LORD your God, am a jealous God who will not tolerate your affection for any other gods.

DEUTERONOMY 5:9

Twelve Scouts

NUMBERS 13–14

God promised to give the Hebrews their own land.
Before they took the land, God told Moses to send
12 scouts to walk through it. Moses chose 12 men
to go. He told them to find out if the people who
lived in the land were strong. He wanted to know
if the cities had big walls around them. He told

them to see what kinds of plants grew there too.

The 12 scouts were gone for 40 days. When they came back, they told everyone what they had seen. They said there were good plants in the land and lots of tasty fruit. But they also said that the people who lived there were giants. And the cities in the land had big, thick walls around them.

Ten of the scouts said that they should not

I learned that ...

God wants me to trust him and have faith in his plan. When he says something is going to happen, it will happen.

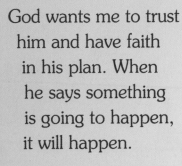

try to take over the land. They were afraid. But two scouts, Joshua and Caleb, trusted God. They said, "Let's go take the land! God is with us. He promised that the land is ours, so he will help us!"

But most of the people did not want to take the land. They agreed with the 10 scouts who were afraid. God was unhappy because they did not have faith in him. So he said the people would have to walk in the desert for 40 years! Except for Joshua and Caleb, none of them would ever enter the land God had promised them.

I can... Take 12 pennies and pretend they are the 12 scouts. Now put them in groups of two. How many groups of two did not trust God? How many groups did trust God?

. . . .

Dear God,
Sometimes it is hard to trust you, especially when I am scared. Help me learn to trust your promises, no matter what. *Amen*

. . . .

Don't be afraid, for I am with you. Don't be discouraged, for I am your God. I will strengthen you and help you. I will hold you up with my victorious right hand.

ISAIAH 41:10

Joshua Fights for Jericho

JOSHUA 6

God told Joshua that he would help the Hebrews take over the city of Jericho. But there was a big wall around the city. God told Joshua exactly what his army should do.

"March around the city once a day for six days," God said. Armed guards and priests would lead the march. More armed guards would follow all the

people. God said everyone should be very quiet while they marched. Then on the seventh day, they would march around the city seven times. the seventh time around, the priests would blow their horns and the people would shout! God said that when that happened, the big wall around the city would fall down. Then Joshua's army could run into the city and win the battle.

I learned that . . .

It is important for me to do exactly what God tells me to do. He knows the best way to do everything.

Joshua's army did exactly what God said. They marched around Jericho once every day for six days. On the seventh day, they marched around it seven times. On the last time around the city walls, Joshua said, "Shout! God has given you the city!" The people shouted, and the walls fell down!

The army destroyed everything inside the city except one woman and her family. She had helped two scouts Joshua sent into Jericho. The scouts promised to protect her, and they did. Joshua's army won the battle of Jericho!

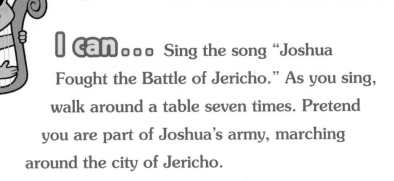

I can... Sing the song "Joshua Fought the Battle of Jericho." As you sing, walk around a table seven times. Pretend you are part of Joshua's army, marching around the city of Jericho.

. . . .

Dear God,
Thank you for telling Joshua exactly what to do. Please help me to do what you say too. *Amen*

SO I PRAY...

. . . .

The LORD your God is indeed God. He is the faithful God who keeps his covenant for a thousand generations and lavishes his unfailing love on those who love him and obey his commands.

DEUTERONOMY 7:9

Gideon's Little Army

JUDGES 7

God chose Gideon to lead an army. They were going to fight God's enemies. Gideon asked men to come be in his army. Thousands of men did! But God said, "Your army is too big. If I let you fight the battle, you will think you won because your

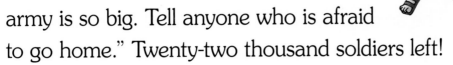

army is so big. Tell anyone who is afraid to go home." Twenty-two thousand soldiers left!

But God said there were still too many soldiers in Gideon's army. So God said, "Take everyone down to the river. Keep the men who cup water in their hands and drink that way." That left only 300 men in Gideon's army.

God told Gideon to give each man a horn and a clay jar. Inside every jar, there was a

I learned that . . .

God doesn't want anyone or anything else to get the credit for the amazing things he does. God wanted Gideon to have a little army so everyone would know God was the reason they won the battle.

burning stick, called a torch. Gideon told his 300 soldiers to divide into three groups. They spread out all around the enemy camp. It was late at night, and everything was dark.

The soldiers watched Gideon. When he gave the signal, every soldier blew his horn and broke his clay jar. All the torches blazed. When the enemy army saw the fire from the torches, they thought a huge army was attacking them! They got scared and ran away. Gideon's little army won without a fight . . . thanks to God!

I can... Make a torch. Roll some yellow or orange paper into a tube shape. Then ask a grown-up to cut slits in one end so it looks like flames. Hide your torch under a bag or a pan. Wait for the signal from your mom or dad, and then pull out your torch!

. . . .

Dear God,
Thank you for using a little army to show how strong you are. I know that your strength and power are all I need! *Amen*

so I PRAY...

. . . .

Honor the LORD, you heavenly beings; honor the LORD for his glory and strength.

PSALM 29:1

143

God Forgives Samson

JUDGES 13:1-24; 16:4-30

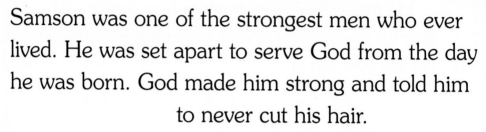

Samson was one of the strongest men who ever lived. He was set apart to serve God from the day he was born. God made him strong and told him to never cut his hair.

Samson destroyed many of God's enemies. The ones who were left wanted to destroy him. They made a plan with Samson's girlfriend. They would pay her a lot of money if she could find out the secret of Samson's strength.

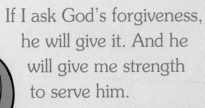

The first time she asked Samson why he was so strong, he lied. He said his strength would be gone if he were tied up with new ropes. But when she tied him up, he broke the ropes. She asked again and again. Each time, he told a different lie.

She kept asking until Samson finally told the truth. If his long hair were cut, it would break his promise to God. Then Samson's

I learned that . . .

If I ask God's forgiveness, he will give it. And he will give me strength to serve him.

strength would be gone. When he fell asleep, she cut his hair. He wasn't strong anymore! His enemies put him in prison.

But then, Samson asked God to forgive him. "Please make me strong just one more time," Samson prayed. God heard Samson's prayer. He forgave Samson and made him strong again. Samson destroyed more of God's enemies that day than he had in his whole life! He died, too, but he died serving God!

I can ... Do exercises to make your muscles stronger. Find a soft place where you won't get hurt if you fall. Can you do jumping jacks? How many? Can you stand on one foot? How long can you do it without falling down?

Dear God,
Thank you that you forgive me when I ask. Thank you for loving me no matter what. Help me to serve you every day. *Amen*

so I PRAY...

If we confess our sins to him, he is faithful and just to forgive us our sins and to cleanse us from all wickedness.

1 JOHN 1:9

Ruth Helps Naomi

BOOK OF RUTH

Naomi and her family moved to a new land because there was no food where they lived. After they moved, Naomi's husband died. She was sad and missed her husband, but she was glad her two sons were with her.

Soon her sons both got married. Naomi was happy and waited for grandchildren to be born. Then something terrible happened. Both of her sons died. Naomi was very sad now.

She decided to go home. Ruth, the wife of one of her sons, went with her. Ruth wanted to stay with Naomi and take care of her. Ruth wanted to serve God like Naomi did.

I learned that . . .

God takes care of us. When we lose things, he likes to give us brand-new blessings!

They went to Bethlehem, but they had no money to buy food. So Ruth went to a field to pick up leftover grain that the workers dropped. Naomi could make bread from the grain.

Boaz, the owner of the field, noticed Ruth. He saw that she took good care of Naomi. He saw that she loved God. He saw that she was kind and nice. Boaz and Ruth got married. They had a baby boy named Obed. He was part of the family Jesus would be born into someday! Ruth and Boaz took care of Naomi. She was happy now!

I can ... Draw a picture of your family. Don't forget grandparents, aunts, uncles, and cousins! Ask your mom or dad to help you spell your family's last name. Write it at the top of your family picture.

Dear God,
Thank you for brand-new blessings, like Ruth's new husband and baby. Thank you for my family! Help us to serve you. *Amen*

Blessed are those who trust in the LORD and have made the LORD their hope and confidence.

JEREMIAH 17:7

The Birth of Samuel

1 SAMUEL 1:1-20

Hannah wanted to be a mother. She wanted it more than anything. But she didn't have any children. She cried and prayed and cried and prayed. But still . . . no baby. Her husband told her it was okay. He loved her very

much and wanted her to be happy.
But Hannah kept crying and asking God for a child.

One day, Hannah and her husband went to honor God at the church tent. Hannah was still sad because she did not have a baby. She cried and prayed to God quietly, in her heart. "God, please give me a son," Hannah prayed. Then she promised that she would give her son to God to serve him.

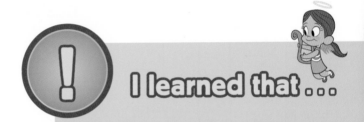

I learned that . . .

God hears our prayers and answers them. Hannah prayed for a long time before Samuel was born. God doesn't mind if we pray for the same thing over and over. We should keep praying, just like Hannah did.

Eli, the priest of the church tent, watched her. He saw that Hannah's lips were moving, but she wasn't making any sound. He went and talked to her. Hannah told him that she was praying for God to give her a son. She cried and told Eli how much she wanted to have a baby. Eli understood and said, "God has heard your prayer."

Hannah felt better. The next day, she and her husband left the church tent and went home. About a year later, she had a baby boy! She named him Samuel. God answered Hannah's prayer and made her a mother!

I can... Sing a soft, bedtime song. Pretend you are singing to baby Samuel to help him sleep. What is your favorite bedtime song?

. . . .

Dear God,
Thank you for hearing Hannah's prayer and answering it. I know you will hear my prayers and answer them, too. *Amen*

. . . .

We are confident that he hears us whenever we ask for anything that pleases him. And since we know he hears us when we make our requests, we also know that he will give us what we ask for.

1 JOHN 5:14–15

God Talks to Samuel

1 SAMUEL 3:1-18

When Samuel was old enough, Hannah kept her promise to God. She gave her son back to God to serve him. She took Samuel to the church tent to live. He would learn how to serve God from Eli the priest. By

this time Eli was very old and could not see very well. Samuel was a good helper for Eli.

One night Samuel was lying in bed when he heard someone say his name. He thought it was Eli calling him. So Samuel ran to Eli and said, "Here I am. What do you need?" But Eli hadn't called him. He told Samuel to go back to bed. A few minutes later, Samuel heard his name

I learned that . . .

God speaks when he has a job for me to do. He may not talk out loud, like he did to Samuel. But God speaks in my heart and through the Bible.

again. So once again, he ran to Eli. But again, Eli said that he had not called him.

Samuel went back to bed. But a few minutes later, he heard his name called again. This time when he went to Eli, the old priest knew what was happening. It was God calling to Samuel! Eli told Samuel to say, "Here I am, Lord. Speak to me. I am listening." Samuel did what Eli told him to do. And God gave Samuel an important message.

I can... Play a listening game. Ask a grown-up to go into the other room and make some sounds. Close your eyes and listen. Do you hear hands clapping? Do you hear a door closing? Do you hear laughing? How many sounds can you name? Take turns making sounds and listening.

. . . .

SO I PRAY...

Dear God,
Thank you for speaking to me when you have a job for me to do. Help me to listen with my heart so I will hear you. *Amen*

. . . .

Be still, and know that I am God! I will be honored by every nation. I will be honored throughout the world.

PSALM 46:10

The People Want a King

1 SAMUEL 10:17-27

Samuel brought all the people of Israel together. He said, "God asked me to tell you this: Remember that he saved you from being slaves in Egypt. Then he saved you from everyone who wanted to hurt you. He always took care of you. But you are still not following him. You

want a king to rule you. You don't
need a king. But you want one, just so you can be
like other nations who do not belong to God."

Samuel told all the people to come together.
They had to
march before
God so he could
pick their king.
God picked the
tribe of Benjamin.
Then he showed
Samuel which
family and finally
which man he
wanted to be
king. The man's
name was Saul.

I learned that . . .

God wanted the people
to be happy with just
him. But they
wanted a king, so
God gave them a
king. They would
find out that life
was best when they
followed only God.

At first the people couldn't find Saul because he was hiding. When they found him, everyone saw that Saul was taller than all the other people! "This is the man God has picked to be your king," Samuel said.

The people were happy and yelled, "Long live the king!" Then Samuel told the people about the king's job. God touched the hearts of some men to become Saul's true friends. But some men made trouble for Saul because they did not like him being king.

I can... Draw a crown and color it. Make it look special! Do you think King Saul's crown looked like yours?

Dear God,
Help me to follow you, no matter what other people do. I want to serve and follow only you! *Amen*

so **I PRAY...**

You must not have any other god but me.

EXODUS 20:3

David Fights a Giant

1 SAMUEL 17:1-51

King Saul and the people of Israel were in a war with their enemies, the Philistines. Both armies had many strong men. But the Philistines had one soldier who was nine feet tall! His name was Goliath.

Every day Goliath shouted to King Saul's army, "Send a soldier out to fight me. I will win for sure! I'm bigger and stronger than all of you. Not even your

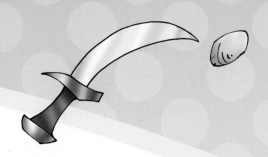

God can beat me!" All God's people were afraid of Goliath. No one would go fight him.

David's older brothers were in King Saul's army. David's father sent him to give his brothers some food. While he was with them, he heard Goliath making fun of God. "That giant can't talk about God like that. I will fight him," David said. "I may be small, but God will help me win!"

Goliath was bigger than anyone David had ever seen! But David trusted God. He grabbed five stones and his sling, a pouch used for throwing stones. Goliath grabbed his big spear and shield. They ran toward each other.

David put a stone in his sling and swung it around. The stone flew through the air. It hit Goliath right on the head! Kerplunk! Goliath the giant crashed to the ground!

I can . . . Find out how tall you are. Ask a grown-up to measure you. Would you like to be as big as Goliath? He was nine feet tall! Was Goliath taller than you are? How many feet taller was he?

Dear God,
Thank you for helping small people do big things. Help me be brave like David and do big things for you! *Amen*

Be strong and
courageous, all you
who put your hope
in the Lord!

PSALM 31:24

David and Jonathan Are Friends

1 SAMUEL 17:55—18:7

David became a hero after he fought Goliath the giant. The whole enemy army ran away after David beat Goliath. Soon, everyone in Israel knew who David was! The people shouted his name. They made up songs

about David's strength and power. Even King Saul asked to meet David. He wanted to get to know the young man who destroyed the giant.

After David talked with King Saul, he met the king's son, Jonathan. David and Jonathan liked each other a lot and became best friends right away! They were almost like brothers because they loved each other very much.

I learned that . . .

Good friends are a gift from God. David and Jonathan promised to be friends forever. I am thankful for my good friends.

From that day on, David lived in the palace with King Saul and Jonathan. The king wanted David close by. He gave David lots of important things to do.

David and Jonathan made a big promise to each other. They promised to be best friends

forever. Jonathan sealed the promise by giving his robe, shirt, and belt to David. He even gave David his sword and his bow and arrows. David and Jonathan would be best friends no matter what!

I can... Give a gift to one of your good friends. Pick something special that your friend will like. Can you draw a picture for your friend? Or can you find a flower or a pretty leaf to give to your friend?

- -

Dear God,
Thank you for my good friends. Help us to love each other like David and Jonathan did. Help me to be a good friend too. *Amen*

- -

A friend is always loyal, and a brother is born to help in time of need.

PROVERBS 17:17

King Solomon's Wisdom

1 KINGS 3

David became Israel's next king. When he got old, his son Solomon became king. Solomon loved God very much.

One night, God came to King Solomon in a dream. God said, "What do you want? Ask, and I will give it to you." Solomon said, "O God, I don't know what to do. I want to be a good king for your people. Give me wisdom so that I can make right decisions and rule the people well." God

was pleased with Solomon's prayer. So he gave Solomon wisdom, and he also gave him money and honor.

Later, two women came to King Solomon. They were fighting over a baby. Each woman said she was the baby's mother. One woman said, "This baby is mine. She took him from me!" The other woman said, "No! He belongs to me!"

I learned that . . .

God was pleased when King Solomon asked for wisdom. We should pray for things that will please God.

King Solomon asked for a sword. He said, "Cut the baby in two. Give half to each woman." One woman cried, "No! Don't hurt him! Let her have the baby." The king wasn't really going to hurt the baby. He only said this to find out who was the baby's true mother. She would rather give up her child than let him get hurt. Now the king knew she was the baby's real mother. So the king gave the baby back to her. When the people heard this, they knew that King Solomon's wisdom was a gift from God.

I can... Pretend you have two cookies and two friends who each want to eat some. But you want to eat some too. How can three people eat two cookies? Can you solve this problem?

. . . .

SO I PRAY...

Dear God,
Thank you for giving Solomon great wisdom. Please give me wisdom too. Help me to use it for your work.
Amen

. . . .

If you need wisdom, ask our generous God, and he will give it to you.

JAMES 1:5

King Solomon Builds God's House

1 KINGS 5—6; 2 CHRONICLES 2:1—5:1

King David wanted to build a big church house for God, called a temple. But God said, "No, David. You will not build my Temple. But your son will

build it instead." So when David's son Solomon became king, he built God's Temple.

Solomon asked one of David's friends, King Hiram, for help. He sent special wood for Solomon to use. Solomon hired thousands and thousands of workers! There were workers to carry supplies, workers to cut stone, and workers to lead other workers.

I learned that . . .

God's Temple was a special place to love and honor him. My church is a special place to love and honor God too.

The whole Temple was built without the sound of a hammer or any kind of tool at the building spot. Special stones were cut before they were brought there. Inside, the Temple walls were covered with wood cut into shapes of angels, trees, and flowers. There was a gold altar and gold lamps and gold cups. Even the doors were gold! There was a very special room in the middle of the Temple. It was called the Most Holy Place.

The walls of that room were covered with pure gold! Solomon made gold chains to protect the opening to the most holy place.

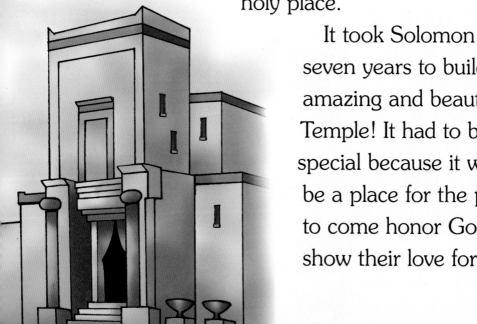

It took Solomon seven years to build this amazing and beautiful Temple! It had to be special because it would be a place for the people to come honor God and show their love for him.

I can ... Draw a picture of your church. Color the whole church golden yellow, like the Temple that Solomon built for God.

· ·

Dear God,
Thank you for my church. Help me to always treat your house with honor and respect. *Amen*

SO I PRAY...

· ·

I was glad when they said to me, "Let us go to the house of the LORD."

PSALM 122:1

179

Ravens Give Elijah Food

1 KINGS 16:29—17:6

King Ahab ruled God's people, the Israelites. But
he was not a good king like David or a wise king
like Solomon. King Ahab was a very bad king.
He didn't follow or honor God. He led the people
away from God. He made fake gods out of stone

and prayed to them. King Ahab did more bad things than all the other kings of Israel before him! God was very angry with King Ahab.

Elijah was God's prophet at that time. He gave people messages from God. So God sent Elijah to King Ahab. Elijah told the king that no rain would fall on the land until God said so. It would be dry for years!

King Ahab got very angry

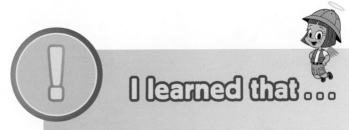

I learned that ...

God gave Elijah a hard job to do. But God took care of Elijah. He sent Elijah to a safe place and gave him food and water. God will take care of me, too!

at Elijah. So God told Elijah to run away and hide near a stream named Kerith. He had to stay right where the stream flowed into the Jordan River.

Elijah obeyed God and went to the Kerith stream. While he was hiding from King Ahab, Elijah could drink water from the stream. But where would he get food? God told big, black birds called ravens to come every day and bring food for Elijah. Every morning and every night, the ravens came and brought bread and meat for him to eat. God took good care of Elijah!

I can . . . Spell the name of the birds that helped Elijah. R-A-V-E-N-S. Ravens are big, black birds. They look a little bit like crows. They make loud sounds that make them sound very brave. Genesis 8:6-7 tells us that a raven was the first bird Noah let out of the ark to see if the flood waters had gone down.

Dear God,
Thank you for taking care of Elijah. You gave him a hard job to do, but you didn't leave him alone. Thank you for taking care of me, too. *Amen*

SO I PRAY...

I love the LORD because he hears my voice and my prayer for mercy.

PSALM 116:1

A Room for God's Helper

2 KINGS 4:8-17

Elisha was God's prophet. He served God and gave people messages from God. One day, Elisha went to the town of Shunem. A very rich woman lived there. She invited Elisha to her home for dinner. From that time on, whenever Elisha went to Shunem, he went to this woman's home to eat. She was very

happy to help God's prophet.

Soon the woman got an idea. "Let's build a little room onto our house for Elisha," she told her husband. "We can put a bed, a table, and a chair in it. Then Elisha will have a place to stay when he comes here. Elisha is a holy man of God. It is good for us to serve him in this way." The woman's husband agreed. So they built the room for Elisha.

The next time Elisha came to

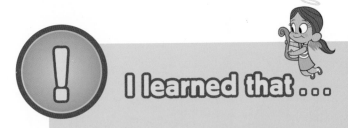

I learned that . . .

God was pleased with the rich woman because she shared what God gave her. It's good for me to share with others too.

Shunem, he stayed in his new room. He was very thankful for it. He wanted to do something nice for the woman to say "thank you." Elisha's servant told him that the woman and her husband wanted a baby, but she had never been able to have one. So Elisha asked God to give them a child. The next year, the woman told everyone that she was going to have a baby! God answered Elisha's prayer!

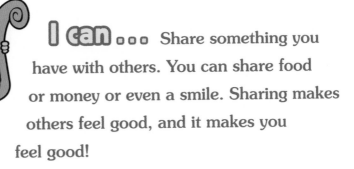

I can... Share something you have with others. You can share food or money or even a smile. Sharing makes others feel good, and it makes you feel good!

Dear God,
Thank you for this story about sharing. You give me lots of good things. Help me to see ways I can share them with others. *Amen*

so I PRAY...

God will generously provide all you need. Then you will always have everything you need and plenty left over to share with others.

2 CORINTHIANS 9:8

Brave Queen Esther

BOOK OF ESTHER

The king of the land was searching for a queen. So he asked all the young women to come to his palace. One was a beautiful Jewish woman named

Esther. She didn't have parents, so her cousin Mordecai took care of her. When Esther went to see the king, Mordecai told her not to tell anyone she was Jewish. The king chose Esther to be his queen!

Later, a bad man named Haman made a new law. Everyone had to bow down when Haman walked by. All the people did, except Mordecai. Haman got angry! He wanted to hurt

I learned that . . .

Esther had to be brave to ask the king for help. But she did it, and God used her to save the Jews. God will use me when I am brave too.

Mordecai. So Haman tricked the king into making a law that would destroy all the Jews. Mordecai sent a message to Queen Esther. "Do something," he said. "This may be the reason God made you queen!"

Esther made a plan to save her people. She invited the king and Haman to a nice dinner. The king was happy and asked Esther what she wanted. He said, "I will give you anything—up to half my kingdom!"

Esther said, "I just want my people saved. Haman is trying to destroy all the Jews. That means me, too, because I am Jewish!" The king was very angry with Haman. He got rid of him and saved Esther, Mordecai, and all the other Jews!

I can ... Be brave like Esther. Is there something you are scared to do? What is it? Are you scared to go into a dark room? Can you take a flashlight to help you be brave? Ask God to help you. It's good to practice being brave.

. . . .

Dear God,
Thank you for how brave Esther was. Help me to be brave when I am scared. Thank you for helping me do things that are scary. *Amen*

. . . .

The LORD is my light and my salvation—so why should I be afraid?

PSALM 27:1

Daniel Does Not Eat the King's Food

DANIEL 1

God's people were not following him. So God let Babylon take over the whole nation of Israel. Strong, young Israelite men were taken away to serve the king of Babylon. The king put these young men in a special program to teach them. They had to learn all about

Babylon. Daniel and three of his friends were in this program. All the young men there were strong, handsome, healthy, and smart. They were treated very well. They even got to eat the king's special food.

But Daniel had a problem with eating the king's special food. So Daniel asked if he and his friends could eat only vegetables and water instead. The guard in charge was

I learned that...

God made Daniel and his friends strong, healthy, and wise. They followed God, and he helped them. Sometimes following God means we will be different from other people. But that's okay. Following God is more important than being the same as everyone else.

worried this would make Daniel and his friends weaker and less healthy than the other young men. If that happened, the guard would be in big trouble. "Just let us try it for 10 days," Daniel said. "If we aren't healthy, then we will eat the king's food." But after 10 days, Daniel and his friends were healthier than everyone else who ate the king's food.

God was pleased with Daniel and his friends. He helped them learn and gave them great wisdom. The king of Babylon saw that they were wiser and stronger than any of his other servants.

I can... Try eating different vegetables, like carrots and broccoli and celery, to find out which one you like best. Which vegetable is your favorite? Why does eating vegetables make you strong?

Dear God,
Thank you for blessing Daniel and his friends. Help me to follow you like they did. *Amen*

SO **I PRAY**...

The LORD leads with unfailing love and faithfulness all who keep his covenant and obey his demands.

PSALM 25:10

Daniel and the Lions

DANIEL 6

The king of Persia had a very big kingdom. He decided to put a ruler over each part and three special rulers over all the others. Daniel was one of these special rulers.

Some men were mad because the king gave Daniel so much power. They wanted to get Daniel into trouble. But Daniel was very honest. They couldn't find anything he did wrong. So they tricked the king into passing a law that would get Daniel in trouble. The law said that people couldn't pray to anyone except the king. They knew that Daniel prayed to God three times every day!

I learned that...

God can keep hungry lions' mouths closed because he has power over all things. God rules over everything, even animals.

Daniel kept praying to God, just like he always had. The men told the king that Daniel had broken the law. The king was sorry, but he couldn't help Daniel. So Daniel was thrown into a pit full of hungry lions. "I hope your God will save you, Daniel!" said the king.

The king was awake all night worrying about Daniel. Early the next morning he ran out to the lions' pit. Did the lions hurt Daniel? No! Daniel was safe! God had closed the mouths of the lions! God saved Daniel because he knew that Daniel had not done anything wrong. The king was so happy that he ordered everyone to pray to Daniel's God!

I can ... Stand on a scale and weigh yourself. How much do you weigh? Lions can weigh as much as 550 pounds! How many of you would it take to weigh as much as the biggest lion?

Dear God,
Thank you that even animals have to do what you say. You are the most powerful! Thank you for keeping Daniel safe. Please keep me safe too. *Amen*

so I PRAY...

All the animals of the earth, all the birds of the sky, all the small animals that scurry along the ground, and all the fish in the sea will look on you with fear and terror. I have placed them in your power.

GENESIS 9:2

A Big Fish Swallows Jonah

BOOK OF JONAH

God wanted Jonah to tell the people of Nineveh that they should start obeying God. But Jonah didn't like the people of Nineveh. He didn't want God to save them. So Jonah ran away. He got on a boat that was sailing away from Nineveh.

Soon God sent a terrible storm. The sailors were afraid, but Jonah was asleep in his room. "Get up!" the captain shouted. "Pray to

your God to save us!"
The sailors tried to figure out who
had made God angry enough to send
this storm. They found out it was Jonah.

"Throw me off the boat, and the storm will
stop," he told them.
The sailors didn't
want to hurt
Jonah, but they
were scared the
storm would sink
their boat. So
they threw
Jonah into the
sea, and the
storm stopped.
Right then
God sent a big

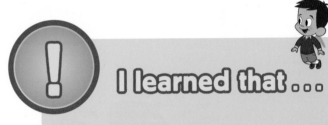

I learned that...

God gave Jonah
a second chance to
do what God told him
to do. God gives me
second chances too.
He never gives up
on me.

fish, and it swallowed Jonah whole! Jonah was inside the tummy of the fish for three days and three nights. He had plenty of time to think about what he had done. "I'm sorry I did not follow you," Jonah prayed. "Give me another chance. I'm ready to go to Nineveh." God told the fish to spit Jonah out. Jonah went to Nineveh to warn the people. They changed their ways, and God forgave them!

I can... Go inside a pretend fish. It must have been a really big fish that could swallow a grown-up man like Jonah. Get a cardboard box, sit inside, and pretend you are Jonah inside the fish's tummy!

. . . .

Dear God,
Thank you for second chances. Thank you for never giving up on people. Please help me to serve you. *Amen*

so **I PRAY...**

. . . .

If someone claims, "I know God," but doesn't obey God's commandments, that person is a liar and is not living in the truth.

1 JOHN 2:4

NEW
TESTAMENT

John's Birth

Zechariah and his wife, Elizabeth, loved God and always tried to serve him. They had prayed many times asking God to give them a child. But now they were both very old and didn't have any children.

One day Zechariah was serving God in the Temple. The priests took turns going in and

burning special oil to honor God. While Zechariah was in the Temple, the angel Gabriel appeared beside him. "God has heard your prayers," Gabriel said. "You and Elizabeth will have a baby boy. You are to name him John. He will help people follow God."

Zechariah didn't believe it. "But my wife and I are very old! How can we have a baby?" he asked.

"God sent me to tell you this

I learned that . . .

God is full of surprises that show just how much he loves you. Nothing is impossible for God! He wanted Elizabeth and Zechariah to have a baby, and he made it happen. Whatever he wants for me will happen too!

good news. But since you have doubted God's messenger, you will not be able to speak until the baby is born!" the angel said. When Zechariah came out of the Temple, he couldn't talk!

Zechariah went home to Elizabeth. She was so happy that they would finally have a child! When the baby was born, everyone asked Zechariah what to name him. Zechariah still couldn't talk, but he wrote down, "His name is John." Right away, Zechariah was able to talk again!

I can... Plan a surprise for someone you love. Then sing about how much you love this person! It's fun to show love to others and make them feel special.

Dear God,
Thank you for surprises that show me how much you love me. I love you, too! Help me to love others. *Amen*

so **I PRAY...**

I will be your God throughout your lifetime—until your hair is white with age. I made you, and I will care for you. I will carry you along and save you.

ISAIAH 46:4

An Angel Has Good News for Mary

LUKE 1:26-38

About six months after the angel Gabriel talked to Zechariah, God gave the angel another job to do. God sent Gabriel to a small town called Nazareth. The angel went there to see a young woman named Mary. She was engaged to be married to

a carpenter named Joseph. He was from
the same family as King David.

"Hello, Mary," the angel said. "Don't be afraid.
I have come to tell you that God is very pleased
with you. He has decided to bless you. You will have a baby boy, and you shall name him Jesus. He will be the Son of God, and he will rule over everything. His Kingdom will last forever."

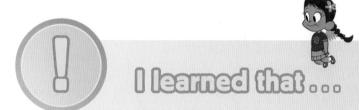

I learned that . . .

God can use anybody
to do his work.
Sometimes he uses
ordinary people to
do very special jobs!
Mary loved God and
wanted to serve him.
God chose Mary to be
the mother of Jesus!

"How can this be possible?" Mary asked. "I am not even married yet. How can I have a baby?"

"The Holy Spirit will come on you," the angel said. "This baby boy will be the Son of God himself. He will be holy. Nothing is impossible with God, Mary."

Mary said, "I am God's servant. I will do whatever he wants. May everything happen just as you have said." After she said that, the angel left.

I can . . . Practice writing the letter "M," the first letter in Mary's name. What letter does your name start with? Can you write that letter too?

- -

Dear God,
Thank you that you use plain old people to do special work for you . . . people like me! I pray that I can do a special job for you someday. *Amen*

so **I PRAY. . .**

- -

Mary responded, "I am the Lord's servant. May everything you have said about me come true."

LUKE 1:38

Baby Jesus Is Born

LUKE 2:1-7

Mary was about to have a baby. She wasn't married, but God's angel Gabriel told her that the baby was God's Son. The angel told Joseph that too. So Joseph knew that it was okay for him and Mary to get married. But before they got married, the ruler of the country had an idea. He decided he wanted to count all the people who lived in his country. He ordered that everyone had to go back to the towns where their families came from. So Joseph and Mary had to travel to Bethlehem to be counted. Joseph came from the family of King David, who had lived in Bethlehem.

When they got there, Bethlehem was filled with people who had come to be counted. Joseph could not find any place for them to stay. There were no open rooms anywhere.

I learned that...

God's Son, Jesus, was born in a barn, not a big palace. That means that God's plan for people to know him is not just for rich people. It is for everyone.

So Joseph and Mary had to spend the night in a barn where the animals stayed. While they were there, the time came for Mary's baby to be born. When the little boy was born, they named him Jesus, just like the angel had said. Mary wrapped baby Jesus in strips of cloth. Then she laid him down to sleep in a feeding trough for animals called a manger.

I can ... Make a birthday card for Jesus! Color it with your favorite colors. We celebrate Jesus' birthday every year on Christmas. Even though today isn't Christmas, sing "Happy Birthday" to Jesus!

Dear God,
Thank you for sending Jesus for everyone. Thank you for loving me that much! *Amen*

For God loved the world so much that he gave his one and only Son, so that everyone who believes in him will not perish but have eternal life.

JOHN 3:16

217

Shepherds Visit Baby Jesus

LUKE 2:8-20

The same night that baby Jesus was born, there were some shepherds nearby. They were guarding their sheep in a field right outside of Bethlehem. In the middle of the dark night, an angel from

God came to them. "I have good news for you," the angel said. "Tonight a baby has been born in Bethlehem. He is the Savior—the Messiah! He will save people from their sins. You will find the baby wrapped in cloth and sleeping in a manger."

Suddenly the sky was filled with a whole choir of angels! They were praising God and saying, "Glory to God in the highest

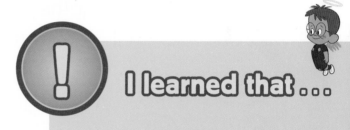

I learned that . . .

God first shared the good news of Jesus' birth with ordinary shepherds—not with kings or rulers. Jesus came for every person! He loves everyone and wants us to know him.

heaven and peace on earth." After they sang, the angels went back to heaven.

The shepherds looked at each other and said, "Let's go to Bethlehem and see this special baby the angel told us about." They ran to the town and found Mary and Joseph and the baby. He was lying in a manger, just as the angel said.

Then the shepherds told everyone they saw about the baby Jesus. Everyone who heard their story was amazed. Mary thought often about everything that had happened. The shepherds went back to their field, but they kept praising God for everything they had heard and seen. It was all just like the angel had told them.

I can... Go on a treasure hunt. Ask a grown-up to hide something and give you clues about how to find it. Pretend you are the shepherds following the clues that the angel gave them to find the baby Jesus.

. . . .

Dear God,
Thank you for sending Jesus for everyone! I'm glad that Jesus came for me! *Amen*

. . . .

I bring you good news that will bring great joy to all people. The Savior—yes, the Messiah, the Lord—has been born today in Bethlehem, the city of David!

LUKE 2:10–11

221

Wise Men Bring Gifts for Jesus

MATTHEW 2:1-12

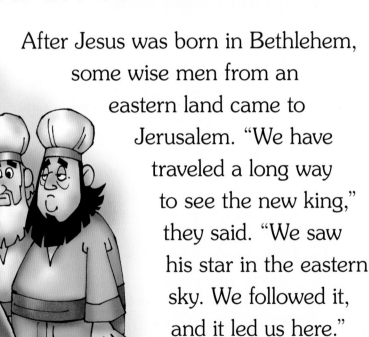

After Jesus was born in Bethlehem, some wise men from an eastern land came to Jerusalem. "We have traveled a long way to see the new king," they said. "We saw his star in the eastern sky. We followed it, and it led us here."

King Herod was not happy to hear that there was a new

king. He called all the priests together and asked where the baby would be born. They told him the new king would be born in Bethlehem. So King Herod called the wise men to his palace.

"Go to Bethlehem and find the new king. But please come back and tell me where he is, so that I may go and honor him too," Herod said.

The wise men left King Herod and went on their way. The star they had followed

I learned that . . .

God celebrated the birth of his Son by putting a special star in the sky. The wise men followed the star to find Jesus. The birth of Jesus was an important thing for the whole world!

guided them to the house in Bethlehem where Jesus lived with Mary and Joseph. The wise men bowed down and honored Jesus. They gave him the gifts they had brought—gold and special oils called frankincense and myrrh. When it was time to leave, God warned them in a dream not to go back to King Herod. So the wise men went home a different way.

I can . . . Name three gifts you could give to a new baby. Count the gifts out loud, "One . . . two . . . three!" The wise men brought three gifts to Jesus—gold, frankincense, and myrrh.

. . . .

Dear God,
Thank you for putting the star in the sky to guide the wise men to Jesus. Thank you for celebrating his birth. And thank you that I can celebrate it too! *Amen*

SO I PRAY...

. . . .

You must love the LORD your God with all your heart, all your soul, and all your strength.

DEUTERONOMY 6:5

Go to Egypt!

MATTHEW 2:13-23

One night after the wise men left to return to their home, God sent an angel to speak to Joseph in a dream. "Hurry! Take the baby Jesus and Mary and go to Egypt," the angel said. "You must go right now! Stay there until I tell you it is safe to return.

Herod is going to try to hurt the baby."
Joseph got up right away. That very night,
Joseph, Mary, and baby Jesus left for Egypt.

Soon Herod found out that the wise men
had gone home
a different
way instead of
coming back to
tell him where
they found the
baby Jesus.
Herod was very
angry. He still
wanted to find
this new king.

So he made
a plan. King

I learned that . . .

God protected his Son,
Jesus, by sending him to
Egypt to keep him safe.
God always protects his
children.

Herod sent soldiers to Bethlehem and told them to get rid of all the little boys there who were two years old and younger. The wise men had told Herod about the star that led them. They said it had appeared about two years before, so the king figured the baby would be about two years old. It was a terrible time in Bethlehem! Herod's soldiers took away all the baby boys. But God protected his Son. Baby Jesus was safe in Egypt. Joseph, Mary, and Jesus stayed in Egypt until King Herod died.

I can ... Talk about a dream you have had. What was it about? Even while we are sleeping, God is watching over us.

Dear God,
Thank you for being a loving Father who keeps his children safe. Thank you for protecting your Son, Jesus. Please protect me, too. *Amen*

The Lord keeps watch over you as you come and go, both now and forever.

PSALM 121:8

The Return to Nazareth

MATTHEW 2:19-23

Joseph, Mary, and Jesus stayed
in Egypt until God told
them it was safe
to leave. Terrible
things happened
to families with
little boys in
Bethlehem
while they were
gone. When
King Herod died,
the danger to
Jesus was past.
So after
King Herod

died, an angel appeared in Joseph's dream again. The angel told Joseph that it was safe to take little Jesus home. "Get up and take Jesus back to Israel. The people who were trying to hurt him are dead now," the angel said.

So Joseph took Mary and Jesus back to Israel. He planned to go back to Bethlehem where they lived before. But then he heard that Herod's son

I learned that . . .

God has a perfect plan. The words of the Old Testament prophets matter to God. He keeps his promises and follows the plan. God is a God of order.

was the new king, and he was afraid of him. He waited for God to tell him what to do. Soon the angel appeared to Joseph again. He told him to take baby Jesus to Nazareth, where Mary and Joseph lived before Jesus was born. This fulfilled a prophecy written about Jesus a long time ago. The prophecy said that the Messiah would be from Nazareth. Everything was happening just like God's plan said it would.

I can . . . Look at a map and find the place where you were born. Ask a grown-up to help you. What's the name of the town where you were born? Is it close to where you live now? Or is it far away?

Dear God,
Thank you for having a perfect plan for everything. Help me to trust your plan. Thank you for always being with me. *Amen*

so I PRAY...

Come close to God, and God will come close to you.

JAMES 4:8

233

Jesus Teaches the Teachers

LUKE 2:41-52

Every year Mary and Joseph went to Jerusalem to celebrate the Passover Festival. The year that Jesus was 12 years old, they went to Jerusalem as usual. After the Festival was over, they left to go home to Nazareth. Jesus wasn't walking with

Mary and Joseph, but they thought he was probably walking with friends.

But that night, they realized Jesus wasn't with any of his friends. Mary and Joseph looked all around, but they couldn't find Jesus anywhere! So they went back to Jerusalem to search for him. They looked everywhere they could think of for three days, but they didn't find him.

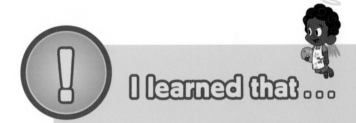

I learned that . . .

Even as a young boy, Jesus was put to work doing what God wanted him to do. That means that I can serve God too, even though I'm young.

Then they heard about a boy in the Temple who was teaching the religious teachers. Mary and Joseph rushed to the Temple. They found Jesus listening to the teachers and talking with them. Everyone was amazed at his wisdom. Mary and Joseph said, "Why did you do this, Jesus? We have been so worried about you. We searched everywhere for you!"

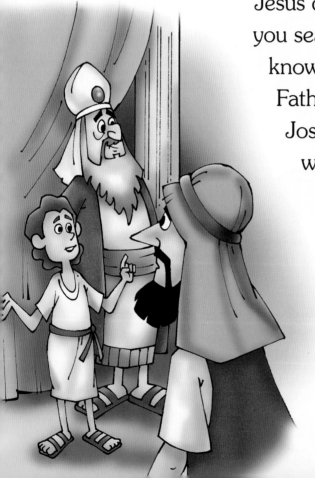

Jesus quietly asked, "Why did you search for me? Didn't you know that I would be in my Father's house?" Mary and Joseph didn't understand what he meant. Jesus went home with them and grew stronger and wiser. Everyone who met Jesus liked him. God was very pleased with him too.

I can... Draw a picture of Jesus teaching in the Temple. Remember to make Jesus shorter than the grown-up teachers. He was only 12 years old!

. . . .

Dear God,
Thank you that people listened to Jesus, even when he was a child. Thank you for protecting Jesus and putting him right to work. Please help me to serve you too! *Amen*

so **I PRAY...**

. . . .

You made me; you created me. Now give me the sense to follow your commands.

PSALM 119:73

Jesus Is Tempted

MATTHEW 4:1-11

The Spirit led Jesus into the desert. For 40 days and 40 nights, Jesus did not eat anything. He got very hungry. One day Satan came and tempted Jesus to turn away from God. Satan is God's enemy. Sometimes he is also called the

devil. Satan is very, very bad. He likes to lie and hurt people.

Satan said to Jesus, "Since you are hungry, why don't you tell these rocks to become bread? If you are really God's Son, you can do it." Jesus answered, "The Bible says that man doesn't live by bread alone but by the words of God."

Then Satan took Jesus to the highest point of the Temple in

I learned that . . .

God understands how you feel when you are tempted to do wrong things. He understands because Jesus was tempted by Satan. God knows how hard it is. He will help you be strong and do the right thing.

Jerusalem. Satan said, "If you are really the Son of God, jump off. The Bible says God will send angels to protect you." Jesus answered, "But the Bible also says that you must not test the Lord your God."

Then Satan took Jesus to the top of a very high mountain. He said, "Look at all the kingdoms of the world. I will give them all to you if you will bow down and worship me." Jesus answered, "Get out of here, Satan! The Bible says to worship God and serve only him!" Then Satan left, and angels came to take care of Jesus.

I can... Make a "sword of the Spirit" out of tinfoil or cardboard. Ephesians 6:17 says that the Bible is our sword. Jesus used the Bible to fight Satan's lies. When you are tempted to do something wrong, remember what Jesus told Satan: "Worship God and serve only him!" Write this verse on your sword.

so I PRAY...

Dear God,
I'm thankful that you understand when I'm tempted to do wrong. Help me to be strong and remember to obey and serve only you. *Amen*

God is faithful. He will not allow the temptation to be more than you can stand. When you are tempted, he will show you a way out so that you can endure.

1 CORINTHIANS 10:13

John the Baptist

MATTHEW 3:1-12; MARK 1:1-8;
LUKE 3:1-18; JOHN 1:19-34

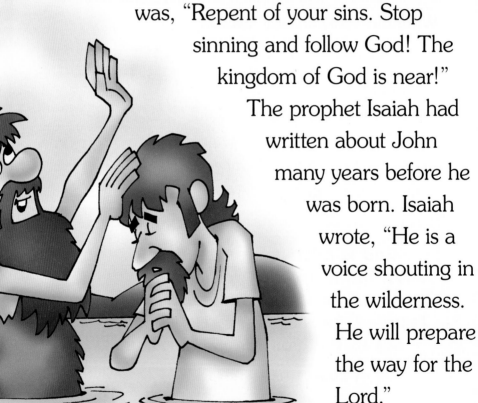

John the Baptist began traveling around preaching about Jesus. His message to the people was, "Repent of your sins. Stop sinning and follow God! The kingdom of God is near!" The prophet Isaiah had written about John many years before he was born. Isaiah wrote, "He is a voice shouting in the wilderness. He will prepare the way for the Lord."

John lived in the desert. He wore clothes made from scratchy camel hair and a leather belt. For food he ate bugs called locusts and honey. People from all over came to hear John preach. After listening to his message, they repented and followed God. Then John baptized them in the Jordan River.

Some of the religious leaders came to hear John's teaching. "Don't just listen to God's Word,"

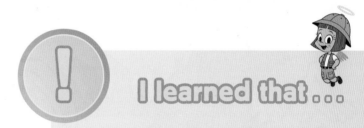

I learned that...

John the Baptist got people ready to hear the messages of Jesus. He told people to stop doing bad things and to follow God.

John told them. "Prove by the way you live that you have repented of your sins and are following God. Every tree that does not give good fruit will be chopped down and thrown into the fire." John told the people that Jesus was coming soon. "The One coming after me is greater than I am. I'm not even worthy to untie his shoes. I baptize you with water. But he will baptize you with the Holy Spirit."

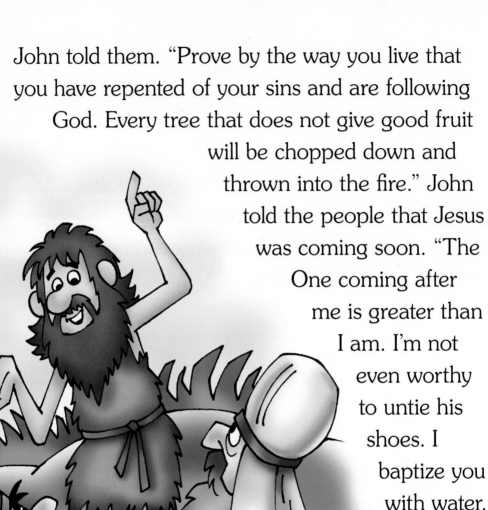

I can . . . Dress up like John the Baptist. Wear a belt like he did. If you have some honey, eat it for a snack, just like John did. We don't eat locusts now, but John ate them all the time. Locusts are bugs that look like grasshoppers and eat plants. In Exodus, locusts were one of the 10 plagues God sent to Egypt.

- -

Dear God,
Thank you for sending John the Baptist to get people ready to hear Jesus' message. I'm thankful for people who remind me to follow you, like my pastor and my Sunday school teacher. Please bless them. *Amen*

SO I PRAY...

- -

If you love me, obey my commandments.

JOHN 14:15

245

John Baptizes Jesus

MATTHEW 3:13-17; MARK 1:9-11; LUKE 3:21-22

John the Baptist was preaching by the Jordan River. Crowds of people came to hear him. He told them that the Kingdom of God was very close. He also told them to stop doing bad things

and to follow God. After hearing what he taught, many people repented of their sins and then asked John to baptize them.

One day Jesus came to the river and asked John to baptize him. But John said, "I can't baptize you. You should be the one who baptizes me! Why are you coming to me?" John said this because he knew Jesus was the perfect Son of God.

I learned that . . .

Jesus was baptized, just like everyone else who loved God. He did things the right way to be our example. Jesus wanted people to see that he followed God's commands too.

Jesus answered, "You must baptize me. Everything must happen exactly as the Scriptures say they will. We must do all that God requires." So John agreed. They stepped into the water of the Jordan River, and John baptized Jesus.

As Jesus came up out of the water, the heavens opened. A dove flew down from the sky and landed on Jesus. The dove was the Holy Spirit. Then a voice from heaven said, "This is my own dear Son. He makes me very happy!"

I can ... Draw a picture of a dove. A dove is a small, gentle bird. Some kinds of doves make a soft, cooing sound. Many times in the Bible, a dove appeared to show that God was there. Put your dove drawing in your room to remind you that God is with you, too.

Dear God,
Thank you for Jesus' example of always doing things the right way. Thank you for being with me all the time. *Amen*

SO I PRAY...

The LORD is close to all who call on him, yes, to all who call on him in truth.

PSALM 145:18

249

Sermon on the Mount

MATTHEW 5—7

One day Jesus went up on the side of a mountain
with his followers. He began to teach them. He
told them that God blesses people who know they
need him. God blesses those who are gentle and
care about others. He is pleased when his children
are lights of his love to those around them.

Jesus also taught his disciples about getting along with others. He taught them to control their anger and love their enemies. He explained that it is very important to help those who don't have as much as you have. But he also said it is good to keep it a secret when you help people, so no one knows except you and God.

Jesus also taught about talking to God in prayer. He said that prayer is not

I learned that . . .

Jesus taught people the best way to live. He told people to always be kind to others. He also taught people to be serious about talking to God and living for him.

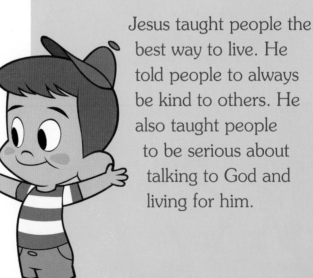

something you should do for other people to see. Prayer is just between you and God. He wants you to pray and to tell him exactly how you feel and what you need. When we pray, we should always thank God too.

Jesus taught that it is important to serve and obey God and pray to him. Jesus also wanted people to know that it is important to treat others with kindness and respect. Living this way helps us to follow God and show love to others. When we do that, our lives are pleasing to God.

I can . . . Sing your favorite song about loving others. If you don't have one, maybe you can make up your own! Do you know the song "This Little Light of Mine"? Jesus wants us to be lights that shine his love to the world!

Dear God,

Thank you for everything Jesus taught about how to get along with others. Help me to do the things you said so I can be a good friend and a good family member. *Amen*

so I PRAY. . .

Keep on asking, and you will receive what you ask for. Keep on seeking, and you will find. Keep on knocking, and the door will be opened to you.

MATTHEW 7:7

Nicodemus Visits Jesus

JOHN 3:1-21

There was a religious leader named Nicodemus. He came to talk to Jesus very late one night. Nicodemus said, "I know that God sent you to teach us. But you say that to have eternal life, I must be born again. What does that mean?"

Jesus answered, "You are a religious leader, and you don't understand these

things? I will explain this to you, but it will be hard for you to understand. You must be born again in the Spirit. What you need to understand is that God loves you very much. He loves you so much that he sent his only Son to earth, so that every person who believes in him will not die but will have eternal life.

"God sent me to save the world, not to judge it. If you trust God, you will not be judged. But those who choose not to believe in God's Son are

I learned that . . .

There is only one way to have a friendship with God and to be able to live with him forever in heaven. That way is to believe that God's Son, Jesus, came to earth, died, and rose again to life. Jesus did all this because he loves us!

255

judged already. That's because they choose to keep on sinning instead of turning away from their sin and living for God."

Jesus is God's one and only Son. He loves us so much that he died to save us from the bad things we do. If we trust Jesus and believe in him, God will forgive us. Then we will live in heaven with Jesus forever!

I can ... Follow these steps to play pattycake with a friend. Sit facing your friend. First, clap your hands once. Then, clap both of your hands with both of your friend's hands. Then clap your hands again. Now try to do it faster! Playing pattycake is easy when you follow these steps. God's way for people to know him is not hard either. You just have to follow the steps.

Dear God,

Thank you for the plan you made so that I can know you. I'm so glad you sent Jesus to save me! Thank you for loving me so much. Please help me to follow Jesus and trust him. *Amen*

so I PRAY...

But God showed his great love for us by sending Christ to die for us while we were still sinners.

ROMANS 5:8

A Woman at the Well

JOHN 4:4-42

Jesus sat down to rest near Jacob's well in Samaria. A woman came to draw water. Jesus asked her for a drink. "You're a Jew, and you're asking a Samaritan for a drink?" the woman said.

Jesus said, "If you knew who you are talking with, you would ask me for living water."

"How will you get water? You don't have a rope or a bucket," the woman said.

"If you drink water from this well, you will get thirsty again. But if you drink the water I give, you will never be thirsty again. My water is a life-giving stream that never runs out," Jesus said.

"Give me some of your water," the woman said.

"First go get your husband," Jesus answered.

I learned that . . .

This woman at the well was good at sharing Jesus' love with people. When she met Jesus and believed that he was the Messiah, she wanted to tell others so that they could know him too!

"I don't have a husband," the woman said.

"I know that. But you have had five husbands," Jesus said.

"You must be a prophet since you know so much about me. There is so much about God that I don't understand. When the Messiah comes, he will explain everything," the woman said.

"I am the Messiah," said Jesus.

The woman left her water jar by the well and ran to town. "Come out to the well," she said. "I met a man who knows everything about me. He is the Messiah!" Many people believed in Jesus that day.

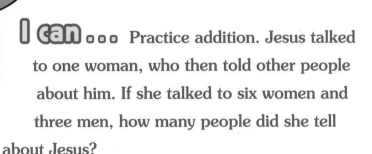

I can ... Practice addition. Jesus talked to one woman, who then told other people about him. If she talked to six women and three men, how many people did she tell about Jesus?

- -

Dear God,
Thank you for people who tell others about your love. Help me to be brave and to share your love with others too! *Amen*

so I PRAY...

- -

[Jesus said,] "I am the way, the truth, and the life. No one can come to the Father except through me."

JOHN 14:6

A Tax Collector Follows Jesus

MATTHEW 9:9-13; MARK 2:14-17; LUKE 5:27-32

Jesus was walking down a road when he saw a tax collector named Matthew. He was sitting in the booth where he collected money from the people. Jesus said to Matthew, "Follow me and be my disciple." Matthew got right up, left everything behind, and followed Jesus. That night Matthew had a big dinner at his house to

honor Jesus. Matthew invited all his tax collector friends to come over and meet Jesus. The religious leaders saw the people who were going into Matthew's house to eat with Jesus. These people were known to be terrible sinners. So the religious leaders went to Jesus' disciples and asked, "Why does your teacher eat with such bad people?"

When Jesus heard them talking to his

disciples, he answered their question himself. "People who are healthy don't need a doctor. Sick people do," he said. He continued, "Think about what I have said. You must learn to be kind and to show mercy. Don't try to make yourself look good by showing off the nice things you do. I have not come for people who already think they are holy. I have come to save those who know they are not good enough."

I can... Find three things in your house that help you feel better when you are sick. How about some cough drops or medicine? Jesus said he was like a doctor who came to help sick people. He makes our souls healthy!

. . . .

Dear God,
Thank you for sending Jesus to save everyone who asks him for help. Please help me to follow Jesus and become more and more like him.
Amen

. . . .

Everyone who calls on the name of the LORD will be saved.

ROMANS 10:13

Jesus Goes Fishing

LUKE 5:1-11

One day Jesus was teaching a crowd of people on the shores of the Sea of Galilee. The crowd got larger and moved in closer to him. Jesus saw two empty boats tied up on the shore. Some

fishermen were cleaning their nets nearby. Jesus got in one of the boats. He asked Simon Peter, the owner, to push the boat a little way out into the water. So Jesus taught the people from the boat.

When he was finished teaching, Jesus said to Simon, "Take your boat out to the deeper water, and put down your nets to catch some fish."

Simon said, "Master, we fished all night

I learned that . . .

Jesus got Simon's attention by using a fishing lesson. Because Simon was a fisherman, that's what made sense to him. Jesus will speak to me in a way I can understand too.

and didn't catch a single thing. But if you say so, I will try again." Simon did what Jesus said. This time, the nets were so full of fish that they started to break! Simon yelled for some other fishermen to come and help. They filled up both boats with fish. There were so many fish that the boats almost sank! Simon was amazed. He fell down on his knees in front of Jesus and said, "Leave me, Master. I'm too much of a sinner to be around you."

Jesus answered, "Don't be afraid. From now on you will fish for people!"

I can ... Sing the song "Fishers of Men." This song reminds us that if we follow Jesus, he promises to make us fishers of men. That means that he will use us to show people God's love.

. . . .

Dear God,
I'm glad that you teach me by using lessons I understand. Thank you for knowing me so well! *Amen*

. . . .

[Jesus said,] "From now on you'll be fishing for people!"

LUKE 5:10

269

Jesus Gathers Some Helpers

MATTHEW 4:18-22; MARK 1:16-20

Jesus started to gather a group of helpers to travel with him and learn from him. These followers were called Jesus' disciples. Jesus chose them to be his special friends and helpers.

One day Jesus was walking along the shores of the Sea of Galilee. He saw two men fishing with a net. They earned their money by fishing. The men were brothers named Simon Peter and Andrew.

Jesus said to them, "Come, follow me and be my disciples. And I will show you how to fish for people!" Right away, both men left their nets and followed Jesus. They didn't ask any questions. They just got up and went with Jesus.

I learned that . . .

When Jesus called people to do his work, they obeyed him right away. They didn't wait until later. They didn't asking any questions. They just followed Jesus. I should do that too.

A little farther up the shore Jesus saw two more brothers, James and John. They were sitting in a boat with their father. These men were also fishermen. They were busy fixing the holes in their fishing nets. Jesus asked these men to follow him too. Right away, James and John both got up and went with Jesus. They didn't ask any questions either. They just left their boat and their father and followed Jesus.

I can... Draw a picture of a fish. These four helpers of Jesus were all fishermen. Hang your picture on your wall to remind you that Jesus has work for you to do too!

. . . .

Dear God,
Thank you that you have special work for each of your followers to do. I want to do things for you! Help me to follow you today. *Amen*

SO I PRAY...

. . . .

[Jesus said,] "If you try to hang on to your life, you will lose it. But if you give up your life for my sake, you will save it."

MATTHEW 16:25

Through the Roof

MARK 2:1-12; LUKE 5:17-26

Jesus traveled around teaching people about following God and serving him. There were always crowds traveling with him, so the news of where he was going spread fast. One day Jesus went into a small home to teach the crowds. The house quickly filled up with people who wanted to listen to Jesus.

Four men came to the house
carrying a mat. Their crippled friend was on
the mat. He couldn't walk at all. The man's friends
had brought him to Jesus to be healed. But they
couldn't get their
friend through the
crowd to Jesus.
So they came up
with a new plan.
They carried
their friend up to
the roof of the
house and made
a big hole in
the roof. Then
they lowered
their friend down
through the

I learned that . . .

Jesus wants us to trust him.
The crippled man and
his friends trusted
Jesus, and Jesus healed
the man so he could
walk! Jesus doesn't
always heal people, but
we can always trust him
to take good care of us.

hole—right in front of Jesus!

Jesus stopped teaching and looked up at the four men. He saw that they had faith in him. Then Jesus turned to the crippled man and said, "Stand up, pick up your mat, and go home!"

The man jumped up! His legs were healed! So he picked up his mat and went home. Everyone in the house was amazed. They praised God and said, "We've never seen anything like this before!"

I can ... Work a puzzle. Puzzles help us learn to solve problems. The four friends figured out a way to solve their problem. They worked together and helped their friend get to Jesus!

Dear God,
Thank you for this amazing story. Help me to trust you like the men in this story did. Thank you for always taking care of me. *Amen*

SO **I PRAY...**

He heals the brokenhearted and bandages their wounds.

PSALM 147:3

277

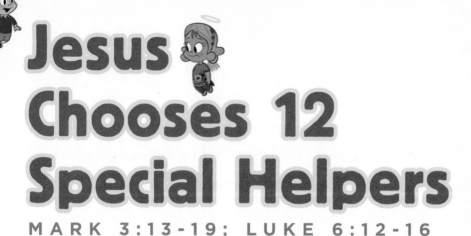

Jesus Chooses 12 Special Helpers

MARK 3:13-19; LUKE 6:12-16

Jesus traveled around teaching about God. People heard about the many sick people he healed and the dead people he raised back to life. Soon large

crowds followed Jesus everywhere he went. Some people wanted to hear him teach. But other people only wanted to see the miracles he did.

One night Jesus got away from the crowds and went off by himself. He wanted to be alone to pray. So he went up on a mountain and prayed to God all night long. The next morning he went back

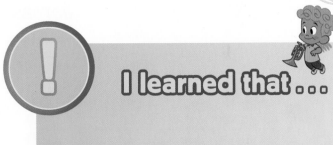

I learned that . . .

Jesus prayed before choosing his closest friends. God helped him see the hearts of these men. Jesus knew that they would follow and serve him. He can see my heart too!

to the crowd of followers. From his big group of followers, Jesus chose 12 men to be his special helpers. They would go everywhere with him and help him teach people about God. Jesus wanted these 12 men to be his closest friends—his disciples. Their names were Simon (Jesus named him Peter), Andrew (Peter's brother), James and John (Jesus nicknamed these two brothers "Sons of Thunder"), Philip, Bartholomew, Matthew, Thomas, James, Thaddaeus, Simon, and Judas Iscariot.

I can ... Thank God for your friends! Friends are a gift from God. Say the names of your friends and what you like about them. Do any of your friends have the same name as one of Jesus' friends?

Dear God,
Thank you that you know what I'm really thinking and how I really feel. Help my heart to always be loving, like yours is. *Amen*

Search me, O God, and know my heart; test me and know my anxious thoughts.

PSALM 139:23

A Widow's Boy Lives Again

LUKE 7:11-17

Jesus and his disciples came to a town called Nain. As usual, there was a big crowd of people following Jesus and watching everything he did. As Jesus came to the gate of the town, he saw some people coming out of the town and crying. It was a funeral group.

The funeral was for a boy who had died. He was the only son of a woman who was a widow. This poor woman had lost her husband and her only son. She was very sad. Many friends were walking with her. They were going with the woman to help her bury her son.

When Jesus saw this sad mother, his heart was filled with care for her. So he stopped the funeral group and said to the

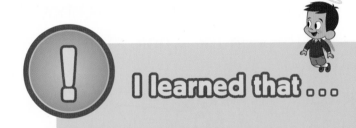

I learned that . . .

Jesus really cared that this woman's son had died. He helped her by bringing her son back to life. Jesus cares about me, too. When I'm sad, he will help me.

woman, "Don't cry." Then Jesus went over to the boy's coffin and touched it. "Young man, get up," he said. Then the boy sat up . . . and started to talk! He was alive again! Jesus gave the boy back to his mother.

The people were amazed. Everyone who saw this praised God and said that they had seen God's hand at work! More and more people heard about Jesus. The news about him kept spreading through the whole area.

I can . . . Wish this boy a happy birthday. He got to have a new birthday when Jesus brought him back to life!

. . . .

Dear God,
Thank you for caring about the things that make me sad, just like you did for the mother in this story. Thank you for loving me so much. *Amen*

. . . .

The LORD is compassionate and merciful, slow to get angry and filled with unfailing love.

PSALM 103:8

The Story of the Seeds

MATTHEW 13:1-23; MARK 4:1-20; LUKE 8:4-15

Jesus liked to tell special stories called parables to help people understand the lessons he was teaching. One parable was about a farmer planting seeds.

As the farmer dropped the seeds, they fell in different places. Some seeds fell on the path. Birds came and ate the seeds before they had a chance to grow. These seeds are like people who hear God's Word but don't understand it. Then the devil takes away the truth planted in their hearts.

Other seeds fell on shallow soil that had rock under it. Those seeds grew into plants very fast. But

I learned that...

God knows what happens in our hearts. He wants us to trust him and tell other people about him. Then we will be like strong plants that grow lots of fruit!

then they died because their roots couldn't get any food or water. This is like people who believe God's Word with joy but don't have deep faith. They give up trusting God when life gets hard.

More seeds fell in thorn bushes. The thorns crowded out the good plants so they couldn't grow or make fruit. This is like people who accept God's Word but let other things in life become more important than God. Instead of serving God, they serve themselves.

Finally, some seeds fell on good soil. Those plants grew strong and healthy. They even grew lots of fruit!

This is like people who believe God's Word, grow strong in their faith, and tell others about Jesus.

I can . . . Ask a grown-up to help you go outside and pull up a weed, like a dandelion. Do you see the plant's roots? Plants begin as little seeds. When the seeds start growing, they grow roots down into the dirt.

Dear God,

Thank you for this lesson about seeds and how people act when they hear about you. I want to be like the plant that fell on good soil. Help me to live for you and grow strong in my faith. *Amen*

SO I PRAY...

[Jesus said,] "Those who listen to my message and believe in God who sent me have eternal life. They will never be condemned for their sins, but they have already passed from death into life."

JOHN 5:24

A Man of Great Faith

MATTHEW 8:5-13; LUKE 7:1-10

One day a Roman military officer came to see Jesus. One of the officer's most important servants was very sick. He couldn't move and was in a lot of pain. The officer asked Jesus to heal his servant. Some Jewish leaders were friends with the officer, so they also asked Jesus to help him. They told Jesus that the officer was a nice man who had done many good things for them. Jesus said, "I will come to your house with you and heal your servant."

Jesus was surprised when the officer said, "Lord, I am not good enough to have you come to my house. You can just say the word, and my servant will be healed. I know this because I am in a place of authority over my soldiers. When I tell them to go somewhere

I learned that . . .

Jesus is pleased when people trust him with all their hearts. This officer trusted Jesus so much that he knew Jesus didn't need to come to his home to heal his servant.

or do something, they do it right away."

Jesus turned to the crowd of people and said, "I haven't seen faith like this in all Israel!" Then he turned back to the officer and said, "Go back home. Because of your amazing faith, your servant is healed." When the officer got home, his servant was all better. He had been healed right when Jesus was talking to the officer.

I can ... Have faith in God! That means trusting that God will always do what's best. Learn to spell the word "faith," F-A-I-T-H. How many letters are in that word?

Dear God,

Thank you for being strong enough to heal this servant from far away. I want to trust you with all my heart, just like this officer did. Help my faith to grow big and strong. *Amen*

SO I PRAY...

Faith is the confidence that what we hope for will actually happen; it gives us assurance about things we cannot see.

HEBREWS 11:1

Jesus Stops a Storm

MATTHEW 8:23-27; MARK 4:35-41; LUKE 8:22-25

One day Jesus was teaching by the side of a lake. As usual, huge crowds of people were all around him. As evening came, Jesus said to his disciples,

"Let's cross to the other side of the lake."
They got into a boat and started across the lake.
Jesus was very tired, so he went to the back of the boat and fell asleep.

When the boat was out in the middle of the lake, a big storm came up. The wind blew very hard, and the waves got higher and higher. Soon the boat began to fill up with water. The disciples were afraid that

I learned that . . .

Jesus has power over everything, even rain and wind. That means I can trust him with everything in my life!

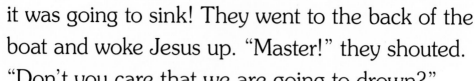

it was going to sink! They went to the back of the boat and woke Jesus up. "Master!" they shouted. "Don't you care that we are going to drown?"

Jesus got up and looked out at the storm. "Be quiet!" he said. Right away, the wind stopped blowing and the waves quieted down. Everything was calm. Then Jesus asked his disciples, "Why are you so afraid? Do you still not have faith in me?"

His disciples were amazed. They asked each other, "Who is this man? Even the wind and the waves obey him!"

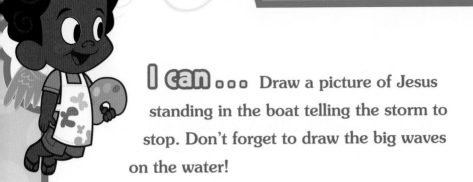

I can... Draw a picture of Jesus standing in the boat telling the storm to stop. Don't forget to draw the big waves on the water!

Dear God,
Thank you for your amazing power. Even storms stop when you tell them to! I'm so glad your power works to take care of me. *Amen*

so I PRAY...

The voice of the LORD is powerful; the voice of the LORD is majestic.

PSALM 29:4

Jesus Helps Jairus's Daughter

MATTHEW 9:18-26; MARK 5:22-43; LUKE 8:41-56

A church leader named Jairus came to Jesus. He fell at Jesus' feet and begged for help. "My daughter is very sick," he said. "But I know you could heal her. Please come to my house." Jesus went with Jairus, and a crowd of people followed them.

A woman in the crowd had been sick for 12 years. She had gone to many doctors, but she was still very sick. The woman believed Jesus could heal her. "If I can just touch his clothes, I know I will be healed," she thought. She reached through the crowd and touched Jesus' robe. Right away, she was healed!

Jesus asked, "Who touched me?" His disciples couldn't believe he asked that. Lots of people were bumping into him. But Jesus knew that healing

I learned that . . .

Jesus does things in his own time. He didn't have to hurry to Jairus's house to help the little girl. Jesus knows the right time for everything.

power had gone out of him. The woman told Jesus what she had done. He said, "Your faith has made you well. Go in peace."

Just then, Jairus's servant arrived and told Jairus that his daughter had died. But Jesus said, "Don't be afraid. Just have faith." They went to Jairus's house where people were sobbing. Jesus said, "Stop crying. The girl is not dead. She is only sleeping." People laughed at him. But when Jesus went to the girl and said, "Get up, little girl," she did!

I can ... Count the miracles in this story. How many people did Jesus help? First, Jesus healed the woman. Then, Jesus brought the girl back to life. This story has two miracles!

· ·

Dear God,
Thank you for your amazing power and love. Thank you that Jesus took care of everyone and didn't have to hurry. Your timing is perfect! Help me to be patient when I have to wait. *Amen*

SO **I PRAY...**

· ·

A prayer offered in faith will heal the sick, and the Lord will make you well.

JAMES 5:15

Dinner for Five Thousand

MATTHEW 14:13-21; MARK 6:30-44;
LUKE 9:10-17; JOHN 6:1-15

Crowds of people followed Jesus everywhere he went. One day a crowd of thousands sat on a hillside listening to him teach. When it was evening, Jesus' disciples said, "Send the people away so they can go buy some food for dinner."

But Jesus said, "No, they don't need to go away. You give them food."

"How can we feed them?" asked the disciples. "We don't have any food, and it would cost a lot to buy food for all these people." There were over five thousand people there!

Then the disciple named Andrew said, "Wait, there is a boy here who has five loaves of bread and two fish. But that's not enough for all these people."

I learned that...

Even a little bit of something is big to God. He can take two fish and five loaves of bread and feed thousands of people! He takes a little money and cares for lots of orphans. God can do anything!

303

"Tell everyone to sit down in groups of 50 people," Jesus said. So everyone sat down. Jesus lifted the bread and fish up to heaven and asked God to bless it. Then he began breaking the bread and fish into pieces. The disciples passed the food out to the people. Every person had all they wanted to eat. Then Jesus told them to gather the extra food so nothing would be wasted. The disciples filled 12 baskets full of leftovers!

I can... Count out 12 crackers. That's a lot! That's how many baskets of food were left over after all the people ate. How many crackers do you have when you just count half of them?

. . . .

Dear God,

I'm glad you can take something small and do big things with it. Thank you for this story of how Jesus took care of the people. Thank you for caring about my needs too. *Amen*

. . . .

This same God who takes care of me will supply all your needs from his glorious riches, which have been given to us in Christ Jesus.

PHILIPPIANS 4:19

Jesus Walks on Water

MATTHEW 14:22-33; MARK 6:45-52; JOHN 6:16-21

Right after Jesus fed the five thousand people, he told his disciples to get in a boat and sail across the lake. Then Jesus sent all the people around him home. After that Jesus went up in the hills by himself to pray.

When his disciples were out in the middle of the lake, a strong storm blew in. Big waves rocked their boat. They had to fight to keep the boat from sinking. About three o'clock in the morning Jesus came toward them. He was walking on top of the water! The disciples were very scared. They thought they were seeing a ghost! But Jesus said, "It's okay! It's me! Don't be afraid."

Peter yelled out to him, "Lord, if it's really you, then tell me to

I learned that . . .

Jesus can give his amazing power to his followers. Peter walked on water with Jesus . . . until his faith got shaky. We need to have great faith to do great things!

come to you by walking on the water." Jesus told him to come. So Peter jumped over the side of the boat and walked on top of the water toward Jesus!

But when Peter looked around at the big waves, he got scared and began to sink into the water. "Save me, Lord!" he shouted.

Jesus quickly grabbed Peter's hand and said, "You don't have much faith, do you?" He helped Peter back into the boat.

Right then, the storm stopped. All the disciples were amazed and said, "You really are the Son of God!"

I can ... Do a little test to see what things float on the top of a bowl of water and what things sink. Does a spoon float? How about a leaf? How about a little plastic toy?

Dear God,
Thank you for being so powerful! It's amazing that you can give such great power to your followers, too. Help me to have enough faith to receive that power. I want to do great things for you. *Amen*

SO I PRAY...

But those who trust in the LORD will find new strength. They will soar high on wings like eagles. They will run and not grow weary. They will walk and not faint.

ISAIAH 40:31

The Good Samaritan

LUKE 10:25-37

One day, a man came to ask Jesus a question. This man knew a lot about religious laws. He asked Jesus how to get eternal life. Jesus reminded him of what Moses taught, "Love the Lord your God with all your heart, all your soul, all your

strength, and all your mind. And love your neighbor as you love yourself."

"Okay," said the man, "but who is my neighbor?"

Jesus told this story: A Jewish man was on a trip when some robbers attacked him. They took his money and his clothes, and they beat him up. Later a priest came down the road. He saw the hurt man

I learned that . . .

God wants me to love people—even people who are different from me. I should look for ways to be kind and helpful.

lying there, but he didn't help him. He just walked around him and kept going. After that a temple worker came by. He saw the man too. But he also went around him and left.

Then a Samaritan man came by. Samaritans and Jews didn't like each other. But the Samaritan felt sorry for the hurt man. He put bandages on the man's cuts. Then he took the man to an inn and paid the owner to take care of the man until he got better.

"Which man was a neighbor to the hurt man?" Jesus asked.

"The one who helped him," the man answered.

"Yes. Now go and follow his example," Jesus said.

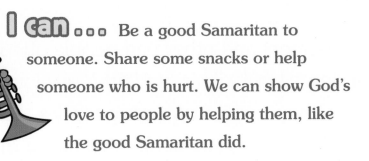

I can ... Be a good Samaritan to someone. Share some snacks or help someone who is hurt. We can show God's love to people by helping them, like the good Samaritan did.

. . . .

Dear God,

Thank you for your love for everyone. Help me to be kind and loving to other people—not just to my friends. Help me to love like you do. *Amen*

SO I PRAY...

. . . .

We love each other because he loved us first.

1 JOHN 4:19

313

The Lost Sheep

LUKE 15:1-7

Tax collectors and other bad people often came to hear Jesus teach. This made the religious leaders angry. They said it was wrong for Jesus to spend time with sinners like people who stole things and told lies.

Jesus heard them saying these things, so he told them this story: "Let's say you had 100 sheep to take care of, but one of those sheep got lost. Wouldn't you leave the other 99 sheep and go look for that lost one? You would search and search until you found it. When you did find it, you would pick up the sheep and carry it home on your shoulders. When you got home, you would call all

I learned that . . .

Every person is important to God. That means that I am important to him! Jesus came to save everyone. But even if I were the only lost person, he still would have come just to save me—just like the good shepherd went to find his one lost sheep.

your neighbors and friends to have a party with you, because you would be so glad your lost sheep was found."

Then Jesus told them what the story meant. "In the same way, there is a bigger party in heaven when one lost sinner follows God than when 99 people who already love God don't stray away from him." God cares about every person. He gets really excited when someone who was lost decides to follow him!

I can . . . Learn to count to 100. If you count one by one, it takes a long time to get to 100. Ask a grown-up to show you how to count by tens like this: 10 . . . 20 . . . 30. Now you can count to 100 a lot faster!

Dear God,
Thank you that I am just as important to you as anyone else. Thank you for loving me so much. *Amen*

SO I PRAY...

There is more joy in heaven over one lost sinner who repents and returns to God than over ninety-nine others who are righteous and haven't strayed away!

LUKE 15:7

Mary and Martha Are Jesus' Friends

LUKE 10:38-42

Jesus and his disciples were on their way to Jerusalem. They came to a small village where a woman named Martha lived. She and her brother and sister were friends of Jesus. Martha welcomed Jesus and his

friends into her home and began
to make dinner for them.

Martha was busy cooking in the kitchen. But
her sister, Mary, sat near Jesus in the other room
and listened to his
teaching. Martha
kept waiting for
Mary to come
and help her with
the cooking . . .
but she didn't.
Finally Martha
went to Jesus
and said, "Lord,
doesn't it seem
unfair to you that
Mary is just sitting

I learned that . . .

God is happy when
people stop doing
things and just
spend time with
him. Being busy
can be good. But
being with Jesus is
the best!

here while I am working so hard to make dinner? Tell her to come and help me."

Martha was surprised by Jesus' answer. He said, "Martha, why are you so worried and upset over these little things? There is only one thing that is really important, and Mary has found it. I will not take it away from her." Jesus was saying that spending time with him was more important than anything else. Even though Martha was working hard, Mary was doing something even better by listening to Jesus.

I can... Answer this question: "What's the best thing we can do?" The answer is, "Spending time with Jesus!"

. . . .

so I PRAY...

Dear God,

Help me to spend more time with you. Thank you for loving me so much. Help me to understand your Word so I can read it every day and talk with you. *Amen*

. . . .

You will keep in perfect peace all who trust in you, all whose thoughts are fixed on you!

ISAIAH 26:3

A Boy Who Ran Away

LUKE 15:11-32

One day Jesus told this story:

A man had two sons. The younger son said, "Give me my part of your money now. I don't want to wait." So the boy took the money and left home. But he wasted all his money on wild living. Soon he had spent everything. Then a famine came over

the land. There was not much food to eat.

The boy got a job caring for some pigs. He got so hungry that even the pigs' food looked good. Finally he thought about the men who worked for his father and had plenty of food to eat.

"I've been so bad that I shouldn't be called my father's son anymore," he thought. "But maybe my father will hire me to work for him." So the boy started walking home.

While the boy was still a long way off, his father

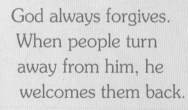

I learned that . . .

God always forgives. When people turn away from him, he welcomes them back.

saw him coming. He ran and hugged him. He was so happy that his son was home! "Let's have a party!" the father said.

But when his older son heard about the party, he was angry. He said, "I've been here all along, but you never had a party for me."

His father answered, "You and I have always been together. But I thought your brother was dead, and he has come back to life! He was lost, but now he is found!"

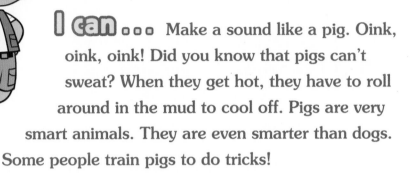

I can... Make a sound like a pig. Oink, oink, oink! Did you know that pigs can't sweat? When they get hot, they have to roll around in the mud to cool off. Pigs are very smart animals. They are even smarter than dogs. Some people train pigs to do tricks!

Dear God,
Thank you for giving us second chances. Help me to forgive people like you do. Thank you for loving me enough to welcome me when I come back to you! *Amen*

No power in the sky above or in the earth below—indeed, nothing in all creation will ever be able to separate us from the love of God that is revealed in Christ Jesus our Lord.

ROMANS 8:39

Lazarus Comes Back to Life

JOHN 11:1-44

Lazarus lived in Bethany with his sisters, Mary and Martha. They were all friends of Jesus. One day Lazarus got very sick. So Mary and Martha sent Jesus a message. They hoped he would come and heal their brother. Jesus loved his friends, but he didn't go to see them right away. He told his disciples

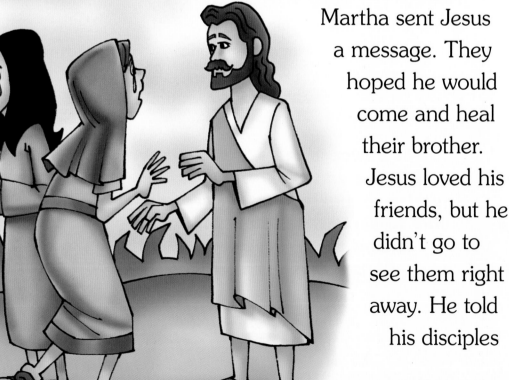

that Lazarus's sickness would not
kill him but would bring glory to God.

A few days later Jesus said that it was time to
go see Lazarus. But by then, Lazarus was dead.
Mary and Martha
were very upset.
When Jesus
came, Martha
said, "If you had
been here, I
know that my
brother would
not have died.
But I know
that God will
give you anything
you ask for now."

I learned that ...

Jesus' main goal
in doing miracles
was to glorify
God. Everything
I do should be
to glorify
God too!

Jesus said, "I am the resurrection and the life."
Then he asked to be taken to Lazarus's grave. It
was a cave with a big stone in front of it. When
Jesus got there, he cried.

"Roll away the stone," Jesus said. "This is
for God's glory." So they rolled away the stone.
"Lazarus, come out!" Jesus shouted. Lazarus
walked out of the tomb. He was still wrapped in
grave cloths, but he was alive! "Unwrap him and
let him go!" Jesus said.

I can ... Use your blocks to build a cave, like the one Lazarus walked out of. Instead of using a big stone to cover the opening, make a cover out of cardboard or cover the opening with a pillow.

. . . .

Dear God,
Thank you for using everything to bring glory to you. I want to bring glory to you too! Help me to do that today. *Amen*

. . . .

LORD, we show our trust in you by obeying your laws; our heart's desire is to glorify your name.

ISAIAH 26:8

Jesus Loves Children

MATTHEW 19:13-15; MARK 10:13-16; LUKE 18:15-17

A big part of Jesus' ministry was teaching people how to live for God and how to treat one another. Everywhere he went, large crowds followed him. Some people wanted to hear him teach. Others wanted him to do things for them, like heal their sick friends or family members. Jesus' days were

always very busy and tiring.

One day, some people came and interrupted Jesus' teaching time. They were parents who had brought their children to see Jesus. They hoped that Jesus would take time to put his hand on the children's heads and pray for them. That was very important to these parents. They believed that Jesus was the Messiah, and they wanted him to bless their children. But

I learned that . . .

Jesus always has time for children. Faith that is simple and trusting, like a child's faith, is what pleases God.

when these parents came up to Jesus, his disciples stopped them. "Don't bother Jesus," they said. "He doesn't have time for your children right now."

Jesus heard what was happening. He said, "Let the little children come to me. Don't stop them! The Kingdom of Heaven is made up of those who are like these children. Their kind of faith is what will get people into heaven." So Jesus put his hands on the children's heads and blessed them.

I can ... Sing the song "Jesus Loves the Little Children." The words "they are precious in his sight" mean that Jesus cares about children and knows they are special. He is never too busy to spend time with children!

* * * * * * * * * * * * * * * * * * * *

Dear God,
Thank you for loving children like me. I'm so glad that childlike faith pleases you. Help me to keep trusting you with simple faith. *Amen*

* * * * * * * * * * * * * * * * * * * *

I tell you the truth, anyone who doesn't receive the Kingdom of God like a child will never enter it.

LUKE 18:17

Jesus Heals 10 Lepers

LUKE 17:11-19

Jesus and his disciples were walking to Jerusalem. As they passed through a village, a group of 10 men were standing away from the road. These men were called lepers because they had a terrible skin disease called leprosy. They had to stay far away from other people so the leprosy wouldn't spread. The lepers yelled out to Jesus, "Master, have mercy on us!"

Jesus looked at them and said, "Go show yourselves to the priests." The 10 men started going toward the Temple. As they went, each man saw that his terrible skin disease had disappeared. They were healed!

Nine of the men ran on into town to show the priest and their families that they were healed. But one man stopped running. He turned around

I learned that . . .

Jesus was happy that the one man came back to thank him for the miracle of being healed. I should always thank God for what he does for me.

and came back to Jesus, shouting "Praise God!"
He fell on the ground at Jesus' feet and thanked
Jesus for healing him.

Jesus said, "Didn't I heal 10 men? Where
are the other nine? Only one has returned to say
thank you? And this one man isn't even a Jew. He
is a Samaritan." Then Jesus told the man to get
up because his faith had made him well.

I can ... List five things that you can thank God for. They can be people or things or animals. It just makes sense to thank God for all he does for you.

* * * * * * * * * * * * * * * *

Dear God,
Thank you for all you do for me. Thank you for loving me. Thank you for my family. Thank you for everything! Help me to remember to thank you every day. *Amen*

SO I PRAY...

* * * * * * * * * * * * * *

Then I will praise God's name with singing, and I will honor him with thanksgiving.

PSALM 69:30

A Blind Man Named Bartimaeus

MARK 10:46-52; LUKE 18:35-43

Jesus and his disciples were leaving the town of
Jericho. A large crowd of people followed them.
A blind beggar man was sitting by the side of the

road. His name was Bartimaeus, but we'll call him Bart for short.

Bart heard the crowd saying that Jesus was walking by. So he began shouting, "Jesus, have mercy on me!"

The people around Bart tried to make him stop shouting. "Be quiet!" they said. "Don't bother Jesus." But Bart kept shouting even louder. He wanted to get Jesus' attention.

I learned that ...

Jesus cares about every person. Even through the noise of the crowd, he heard Bartimaeus calling to him. When I call to Jesus, he hears me, too.

Even though the crowd told Bart to be quiet, Jesus heard him. So he stopped and said, "Tell that man to come over here."

All the people around Bart said, "Go on. He wants to see you. Get up! He is calling you." Bart jumped up and went to Jesus.

"What do you want me to do for you?" Jesus asked.

"Lord, I want to see," Bart answered.

"Go on your way," Jesus said. "Your faith has healed you." Right away, Bart was able to see. He wasn't blind anymore! Bart followed Jesus down the road, praising God. All the people who saw this miracle praised God too.

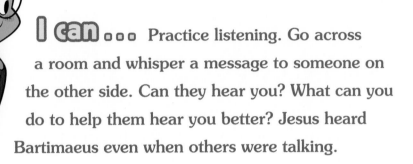

I can ... Practice listening. Go across a room and whisper a message to someone on the other side. Can they hear you? What can you do to help them hear you better? Jesus heard Bartimaeus even when others were talking.

Dear God,
Thank you for hearing every voice that calls to you. Thank you for hearing my prayers and for answering them. *Amen*

The Lord has heard my plea;
the Lord will answer my prayer.

PSALM 6:9

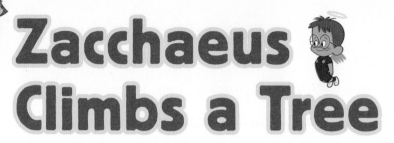

Zacchaeus Climbs a Tree

LUKE 19:1-10

Jesus was walking through the town of Jericho. As usual, a large crowd was all around him. There was a man in Jericho named Zacchaeus. He was a very important tax collector and was very rich. But most people didn't like tax collectors because they often cheated the people to get more of their money.

Zacchaeus wanted to see Jesus. But he was a very short man. He could not see over the taller

people in the crowd. So Zacchaeus ran ahead of the crowd. Then he climbed up into a sycamore tree so that he could see Jesus.

When Jesus passed below the tree, he looked up and said, "Zacchaeus! Come down. I want to come to your house today." So Zacchaeus climbed down fast and went home to serve dinner to Jesus. Zacchaeus was very happy and excited!

I learned that . . .

When someone meets Jesus, that person's heart changes. Jesus gives people new hearts that want to do the right thing.

But the people were not. They were angry that Jesus was spending time with a bad tax collector! They didn't know that Zacchaeus had changed. He promised Jesus that he would give half his money to the poor. He would also pay back everyone he had cheated. He would even pay them four times more than he owed them! Jesus was happy. He knew that Zacchaeus believed in him now and would be honest and fair.

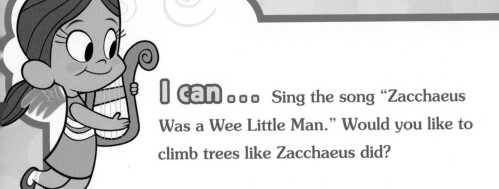

I can... Sing the song "Zacchaeus Was a Wee Little Man." Would you like to climb trees like Zacchaeus did?

Dear God,
Thank you for changing people's hearts when they meet you. Thank you that anyone can change because of your power! Amen

SO I PRAY...

The LORD your God will change your heart and the hearts of all your descendants, so that you will love him with all your heart and soul and so you may live!

DEUTERONOMY 30:6

The Unforgiving Debtor

MATTHEW 18:21-35

One time Peter asked Jesus, "Lord, how often must I forgive someone who wrongs me? Is seven times enough?"

Jesus answered, "No. Seventy times seven!" Then he told this story:

One man owed the king millions of dollars. But the man didn't have the money. So the king ordered that the man, his wife, and his children be sold to pay the debt. The man begged the king to forgive him and asked for more time to pay the debt. The king felt bad for him. So he forgave the whole debt and told the man he didn't have to pay anything!

After this, the man went to another man who owed him

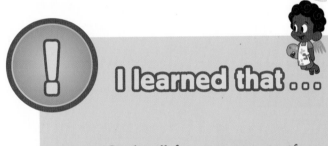

I learned that...

God will forgive my sin if I ask and if I am truly sorry for the wrong things I've done. He wants me to forgive those who hurt me, too.

a small debt. He grabbed the man by the shirt and told him to pay the money right away. The man couldn't pay it and asked for more time. But the first man put him in jail until he could pay. The king heard about this and got angry.

The king said to the unforgiving man, "I forgave the huge amount you owed me, but you put another man in prison for a small amount." Then the king sent the unforgiving man to prison until he paid every cent.

Then Jesus said, "God will do this to you if you don't forgive others."

I can... Make a card for someone you have hurt. Draw a nice picture on the front and write your name on the inside. Give the card to the person you hurt. Say you are sorry and ask the person to forgive you.

Dear God,
Thank you for forgiving my sins.
I really am sorry for the wrong things
I do. Please forgive me. Help me to
forgive those who hurt me, too. *Amen*

so **I PRAY...**

Oh, what joy for those whose disobedience is forgiven, whose sins are put out of sight.

ROMANS 4:7

The 10 Servants

LUKE 19:11-27

Jesus decided to teach about how we should use the gifts God gives us. So he told this story:

A rich man had to go to a land far away where he would be crowned king. Before he left, he talked to his 10 servants. He gave each of them one pound of silver to invest for him. He wanted them to use that money to make more money.

When the king returned, he asked the 10 servants what they had done with his money. The first servant had made 10 times more money than what he had been given. "Well done!" the king said. He made that servant a ruler. The next servant had earned five times more money. The king made him a ruler too.

But the third servant only brought back the same

I learned that ...

God wants me to use the gifts and talents he has given me. If I use them well, then he will give me even more chances to use them.

money the king gave him. He told the king that he was afraid to use the king's money, so he just hid it. The king was very angry. He took the money away from that servant and gave it to the first servant who had the most money. The king said, "Those who use well what they are given will get even more. But those who don't use what they are given will lose even what they do have."

I can ... Name five things that you are good at doing and like to do. Do you have fun running or climbing? Do you like to build things? Are you good at singing? Those are your gifts and talents! God wants you to use them.

Dear God,
Thank you for giving me things I'm good at doing. Help me to do them for your honor and glory. *Amen*

SO I PRAY...

Be very careful to obey all the commands and the instructions that Moses gave to you. Love the LORD your God, walk in all his ways, obey his commands, hold firmly to him, and serve him with all your heart and all your soul.

JOSHUA 22:5

Jesus Rides into Jerusalem

MATTHEW 21:1-11; MARK 11:1-11;
LUKE 19:28-40; JOHN 12:12-19

Jesus and his disciples were going to the city of
Jerusalem. They walked until
they got to a small
town outside of the
city. They stopped
there. Jesus
told two of his
followers to
go on ahead
of the others.
He said,
"Right after
you enter
the city, you

will see a young colt tied up. It has never been ridden. Untie it and bring it to me. If anyone asks you why you are taking it, just say that the Lord needs it."

So the two men went into the city. They found the colt, just as Jesus said. When the owner asked why they were taking it, they told him that the Lord needed it. He let them go with no more

I learned that . . .

It is good to worship and praise God. He is pleased when I praise him in front of other people.

questions. Jesus' friends put their coats over the colt. Jesus sat on it to ride into Jerusalem.

Crowds of people stood along the road as Jesus rode by. Many of them spread their coats on the road so the colt could walk on them.

Some people cut branches from palm trees and spread them on the road too. It was like a parade, with Jesus in the middle. People all around him shouted, "Bless the King who comes in the name of the Lord! Praise God in highest heaven!"

I can ... Pretend you are a colt. Crawl around the floor on your hands and knees and say, "hee haw." Colts are baby boy donkeys. Baby girl donkeys are called fillies. Donkeys are smaller than horses but are very strong. That's why a little colt could carry Jesus on his back.

· ·

Dear God,
Thank you for sending Jesus to be our King. Thank you for this story about people praising him. I want to praise the King too! *Amen*

· ·

Praise God for the Son of David!
Blessings on the one who comes
in the name of the LORD! Praise
God in highest heaven!

MATTHEW 21:9

A Woman Anoints Jesus' Feet

JOHN 12:1-8

It was six days before the Passover celebration.
The religious leaders were looking for a chance to
trap Jesus. They wanted to get rid of him.

Jesus was in Bethany at the home of a man named Lazarus—the same man Jesus had raised from the dead. Jesus and his friends were having dinner at Lazarus's house. His sisters, Mary and Martha, were there too.

Mary came to Jesus carrying a beautiful jar filled with very special perfume. It cost a lot of money. Mary opened the jar and poured the perfume over

I learned that . . .

Worshiping Jesus brings him joy! Jesus is proud of us when we do special things to show we love him. Mary honored Jesus by pouring the perfume on him.

Jesus' feet. Then she wiped his feet with her hair.

One of Jesus' disciples named Judas got angry. He said, "That perfume cost so much money! She should have sold it and given the money to the poor."

Jesus said, "Leave her alone. Don't yell at her for doing such a good thing for me. There will always be poor people who need help. But I will not be here with you for much longer. This woman has anointed my body. She is getting me ready to be buried."

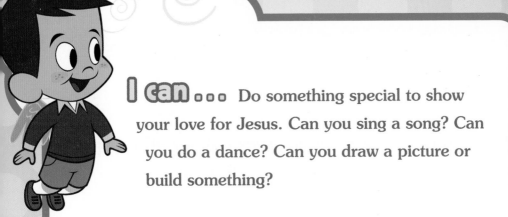

I can... Do something special to show your love for Jesus. Can you sing a song? Can you do a dance? Can you draw a picture or build something?

. . . .

Dear God,
Thank you for this story about worshiping you. I want to do special things for you too. Help me to worship you more and more. *Amen*

. . . .

Honor the LORD for the glory of his name. Worship the LORD in the splendor of his holiness.

PSALM 29:2

The Last Supper

MATTHEW 26:17-30; MARK 14:12-26; LUKE 22:7-30

Jesus and his 12 disciples were all together, getting
ready to eat the Passover meal. That evening,
Jesus sat down at the table with his friends.
While they were eating,
Jesus said, "One of
you is going to
betray me."

Jesus meant that one of them would help Jesus' enemies hurt him. His friends were very upset. Each one asked Jesus, "Is it me? Am I the one?"

Jesus said, "One of you will betray me, just as the Scriptures say. It would be better for that man if he had never been born."

Judas, the one who would betray him, asked, "Teacher, am I the one?"

I learned that . . .

Everything Jesus did, he did because he loved me. He wants me to remember all he did and to be thankful for it.

Jesus answered, "You are."

Then Jesus took some bread and asked God to bless it. He broke it into pieces and gave it to his friends. He said, "Eat this, and think of my body that is given for you." Then he took the wine and gave thanks for it. He passed it around to his friends and said, "Drink this, and think of my blood that is poured out for you. It will seal the promise God made to forgive the sins of many. Do this to remember me." Jesus and the disciples sang a hymn together and left for the garden of Gethsemane.

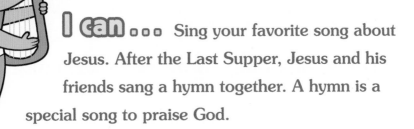

I can ... Sing your favorite song about Jesus. After the Last Supper, Jesus and his friends sang a hymn together. A hymn is a special song to praise God.

. . . .

Dear God,

Thank you for sending Jesus to die for my sins. Thank you for loving me that much. Help me to always remember what Jesus did for me. *Amen*

. . . .

This is real love—not that we loved God, but that he loved us and sent his Son as a sacrifice to take away our sins.

1 JOHN 4:10

Jesus Prays in a Garden

MATTHEW 26:36-46; MARK 14:32-42; LUKE 22:39-46

Jesus took 11 of his disciples to a garden named
Gethsemane. Judas had already left the group.
Jesus told his friends to sit together while he went

ahead to pray. He took Peter, James, and John with him. Jesus was very upset. He told them, "My soul is filled with pain and sadness. Stay here and watch with me."

He went a little farther away from them and fell to the ground, praying, "Father, everything is possible for you. If there is any other way to do things, please do it. But still I want your will to be done, not mine."

I learned that ...

Jesus wanted his friends to help him by praying. It is important to have friends to pray with you and for you.

When he was finished praying, he went back to Peter, James, and John. They had fallen asleep. Jesus woke them and said, "Couldn't you stay awake with me for even one hour? Keep watch and pray!" Then he went away and prayed some more. He was so upset that he started sweating drops of blood.

When Jesus returned, they were asleep again. He woke them up and asked them to keep watch. Jesus went away to pray a third time. When he returned, they were asleep again! "Go ahead and sleep," he said. "The time has come. I am betrayed into the hands of sinners."

I can... Count out 11 crackers. That's how many disciples went to the garden with Jesus. Now count out just three crackers. That's how many of his friends Jesus took with him to pray.

. . . .

Dear God,

I wish Jesus' friends had prayed for him instead of sleeping. Help me remember to pray for my friends. I want to be there for them no matter what they need. Thank you for always hearing our prayers. *Amen*

SO I PRAY...

. . . .

The earnest prayer of a righteous person has great power and produces wonderful results.

JAMES 5:16

Jesus Dies on the Cross

MATTHEW 27:32-56; MARK 15:21-41;
LUKE 23:26-49; JOHN 19:17-30

Jesus' enemies wanted to get rid of him. They lied and got Jesus arrested, even though he didn't do anything wrong. They said he should be put to death. He would die by being crucified on a cross.

They beat Jesus up and made fun of him. Then

soldiers took him to a hill called Golgotha, where they crucified criminals. Jesus had to carry the heavy, wooden cross that he would die on. But he was so weak from getting beaten up that he could barely walk. The soldiers pulled a man named Simon from the crowd. They made him carry Jesus' cross.

At Golgotha, the soldiers nailed Jesus' hands and

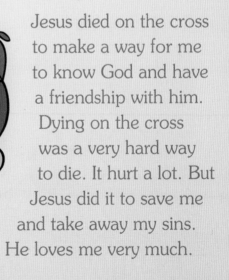

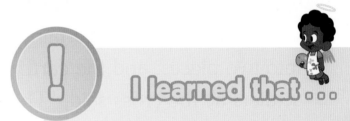

I learned that . . .

Jesus died on the cross to make a way for me to know God and have a friendship with him. Dying on the cross was a very hard way to die. It hurt a lot. But Jesus did it to save me and take away my sins. He loves me very much.

feet to the cross. They put a sign over his head that said, "King of the Jews." Two criminals were crucified at the same time, one on either side of Jesus. People passing by shouted at Jesus, "Hey, if you are the Son of God, save yourself and come down from the cross."

At noon the sky went dark and stayed dark for three hours. Jesus cried out, "My God, my God, why have you left me?" Then he died. At that very minute the huge curtain in the Temple tore into two pieces, and the earth shook. Some of the soldiers by the cross said, "This man really was the Son of God."

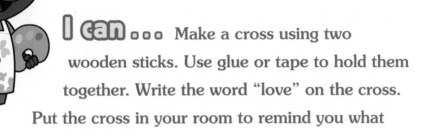

I can... Make a cross using two wooden sticks. Use glue or tape to hold them together. Write the word "love" on the cross. Put the cross in your room to remind you what Jesus did for you.

· ·

Dear God,
Thank you for loving me so much! Thank you for all Jesus did for me and still does for me every day. I love you. *Amen*

so **I PRAY...**

· ·

Christ died for us so that, whether we are dead or alive when he returns, we can live with him forever.

1 THESSALONIANS 5:10

Jesus Has Risen!

MATTHEW 28:1-10; MARK 16:1-8; LUKE 24:1-12

Jesus was crucified on a Friday. After he died, he was buried in the tomb of a man named Joseph. It was a cave. The soldiers rolled a big stone in front of the opening so it was sealed shut.

Early on Sunday morning, some women went to the tomb. They were going to put oil and spices on Jesus' body. That was a way people showed how much they loved the person who had died. The women were worried about how they would move the big stone that covered the opening of the tomb.

But when they got there, the stone had already been moved. An angel was inside

I learned that . . .

God is more powerful than death. He brought Jesus back to life! He promises that I can live forever too, if I am his child.

the tomb! His face shone like lightning, and his clothes were white as snow. The angel said, "I know you are looking for Jesus. He isn't here! He has risen back to life, just as he said he would. Come over here and see where his body was lying. Now go tell his disciples that he is risen!"

The women were filled with joy! They ran back to town to tell the disciples that Jesus was alive! Some of the disciples ran back to the tomb to look. Peter ran inside it. He saw the cloth that had been wrapped around Jesus. But Jesus wasn't there. He had risen!

I can... Make a cave out of a shoe box. Cut a piece of paper into a circle big enough to cover the opening of your cave. Use some white paper to make an angel, and put him inside the cave.

Dear God,
Thank you for bringing Jesus back to life! I'm glad you are stronger than death. Thank you that I can live forever because Jesus died and rose again! *Amen*

The angel said, "Don't be alarmed. You are looking for Jesus of Nazareth, who was crucified. He isn't here! He is risen from the dead! Look, this is where they laid his body."

MARK 16:6

The Road to Emmaus

LUKE 24:13-34

The same day that Jesus rose from the dead, two of his followers were walking to Emmaus. As they walked, they talked about everything that had happened. Suddenly Jesus himself was walking with them! But God kept them from knowing it was Jesus.

Jesus asked what they were talking about. The men both

looked very sad. One of them said, "You must be the only person in Jerusalem who doesn't know what things have happened."

"What things?" Jesus asked.

"The things that happened to Jesus of Nazareth," the men said. "He was a wonderful teacher. But the religious leaders didn't like him. He was crucified. We thought he was the Messiah who would save

I learned that . . .

God has to open our eyes for us to know him. The men on the road didn't know who Jesus was until he wanted them to.

us. Some women went to his tomb this morning, but his body was gone!"

Jesus said, "Didn't he tell you that he would rise back to life?" Then he quoted Scripture verses about himself.

When they got to Emmaus, they asked Jesus to eat with them. They still didn't know it was him. As Jesus sat down, suddenly the two men knew who he was! But then Jesus disappeared! The two men said, "Didn't our hearts feel warm when he talked with us?" They went back to Jerusalem to tell Jesus' other followers that they had seen him. "The Lord has really risen!" the followers said.

I can... Tell people about Jesus. Then ask God to open their eyes so they can see him and know who he is.

. . . .

Dear God,
Thank you for opening the eyes of the two men in this story so they could see you. I want to see you and know you more. Help others to see you too.
Amen

. . . .

I want to know Christ and experience the mighty power that raised him from the dead.

PHILIPPIANS 3:10

Jesus Goes Back to Heaven

MARK 16:9-20; LUKE 24:35-53; ACTS 1:6-11

The two men who saw Jesus on the road to Emmaus told some of Jesus' other friends about seeing him. As they were talking, Jesus was suddenly standing there in the room with them! He said, "Peace be with you." But everyone in the room was very scared because they thought he was a ghost.

"Why are you afraid?" Jesus asked

them. "Don't you know it's me? Look at my hands. Look at my feet. You can see where the nails were, so you can know it is really me. Touch me. Ghosts don't have bodies, but I do." Jesus' friends still weren't sure. So Jesus asked if they had any food. They gave him some fish, and he ate it!

Jesus said, "When I was with you, I told you all about what the prophets wrote about me.

I learned that . . .

Jesus gave his followers a job—go and tell everyone how much he loves them. It's good news, and we should share it!

They wrote that the Messiah must suffer, die, and rise again. This had to happen so people could be saved from their sins. Now go in my power and take this message to everyone. Go into the whole world and tell people this good news! Teach them that God will forgive their sins if they repent. I will send the Holy Spirit to help you." Then Jesus lifted his hands, and he was taken up to heaven!

I can . . . Take a flashlight into a dark room. Turn it on and off a few times. Can you see better when the flashlight is on or off? Jesus wants us to be lights in a dark world—just like a flashlight in a dark room! When we love people, we help them see Jesus better.

Dear God,
Thank you that Jesus came back to life. Help me to be a light to help people see Jesus better. Thank you for the promise of living forever with Jesus in heaven! *Amen*

SO I PRAY...

[Jesus said,] "Teach these new disciples to obey all the commands I have given you. And be sure of this: I am with you always, even to the end of the age."

MATTHEW 28:20

The Holy Spirit Comes

ACTS 2:1-41

Seven weeks after Jesus went up to heaven,
a group of believers were together in one room.
Suddenly a strange sound came from heaven.
It sounded like a powerful windstorm. It was so
loud that it filled the room. Then little things that

looked like small flames of fire appeared above every person's head. Every person in the room was filled with the power of the Holy Spirit! They all began speaking in new languages—languages they had never known before. They could do this because of the power of the Holy Spirit.

Some people were visiting Jerusalem from other lands. When they heard their own languages

I learned that . . .

The Holy Spirit is a special gift from God. He lives in our hearts to remind us to follow God. He helps us to do the right thing.

being spoken, they were amazed! "How can these people know our languages?" they asked. "They are all from this land, not from our countries!"

Then Peter stood up. He explained that the power of the Holy Spirit was working. That's why the believers could speak languages they didn't know. Peter told the crowd all about Jesus. He said, "Each of you must stop sinning. Then turn to God and follow him. God will forgive your sins because of Jesus Christ. Then you will get the gift of the Holy Spirit too!" Peter kept preaching for a long time. About three thousand people believed in Jesus that day!

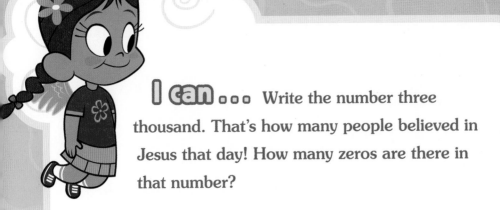

I can... Write the number three thousand. That's how many people believed in Jesus that day! How many zeros are there in that number?

Dear God,
Thank you for the gift of the Holy Spirit. I'm glad you are always with me. *Amen*

When you believed in Christ, he identified you as his own by giving you the Holy Spirit, whom he promised long ago.

EPHESIANS 1:13

Peter and John Heal a Lame Man

ACTS 3:1-11

One day Peter and John went to the Temple for the prayer service. There was a prayer service at the Temple every afternoon at three o'clock. There was a crippled man sitting by the Temple gate called Beautiful Gate. This man's friends carried him there

every day so he could beg
for money. His whole life, this man had never
been able to walk.

When the crippled man saw Peter and John,
he asked them for some money. But Peter said to
the man, "Look
at me. I have
something better
than money for
you. In the name
of Jesus Christ,
get up and walk!"

Then Peter
took the man by
the hand and
helped him get
up. As the man
stood, right away
his legs and

I learned that . . .

Peter knew he had
something better than
money to give the
crippled man. God
gave Peter the power
to heal the man! For
the first time in his life,
the man could walk!

ankles were healed, and strength came into them. The man started walking around, jumping, and praising God! He was so happy and excited!

The man went inside the Temple with Peter and John. People saw him walking around and heard him praising God. They knew he was the same man who had been crippled, because they had seen him sitting by the Temple gate every day. They were all amazed that he was healed! It was a miracle!

I can... Jump up and down like the man in the story. How far can you jump? Kangaroos can go 25 feet in one jump! They can't move their legs one at a time, so they have to hop everywhere on two legs.

Dear God,
Thank you for giving your power to all your followers. Thank you for letting Peter heal this man so he could walk and jump! Help me to praise you like he did. *Amen*

SO I PRAY...

We now have this light shining in our hearts, but we ourselves are like fragile clay jars containing this great treasure. This makes it clear that our great power is from God, not from ourselves.

2 CORINTHIANS 4:7

393

Saul Becomes Jesus' Friend

ACTS 9:1-20

Saul did not like Christians. He hurt all the Christians in his town. Then he went to Damascus so he could hurt the Christians there, too. Saul wouldn't be happy until all the Christians were in jail!

As Saul and his friends were walking to Damascus, a bright light from heaven suddenly came and shone down around him. Saul fell to the ground. He heard a voice from heaven ask, "Saul, why are you hurting me?"

Saul asked, "Who are you?"

The voice answered, "I'm Jesus, the one you are hurting. Now get up and go into the city. Someone will tell you what to do." The men who were walking with Saul were scared.

I learned that...

God can change people. Saul went from hurting Christians to teaching about Jesus all the time!

They heard the voice speaking, but they didn't see anyone! When Saul got up, he couldn't see anything. He was blind! So his friends had to lead him to Damascus. He was blind for three days and didn't eat or drink anything.

In Damascus a man named Ananias came to see Saul. Ananias said, "Jesus sent me to you so that you can get your sight back." He put his hands on Saul. Right away, something that looked like scales or scabs fell from Saul's eyes. He could see again! After that, Saul spent all his time teaching about Jesus and telling people, "He is truly the Son of God!"

I can . . . Pretend you are blind, like Saul was for three days. Ask a grown-up to tie a cloth over your eyes so you can't see. Then ask someone to lead you around without bumping into things.

. . . .

Dear God,
Thank you that you can change people.
Thank you for Saul and how excited
he was to teach about you! *Amen*

so I PRAY...

. . . .

*So all of us who have had that veil
removed can see and reflect the
glory of the Lord. And the Lord—who
is the Spirit—makes us more and
more like him as we are changed
into his glorious image.*

2 CORINTHIANS 3:18

Saul Escapes in a Basket

ACTS 9:23-25

After Saul believed in Jesus, he spent all his time and energy teaching and preaching about him. He was just as excited about helping people to believe in Jesus as he had been about stopping people from believing in Jesus before. Some of Saul's old

friends were angry with him for believing in Jesus. They had worked with Saul to stop the spread of Christianity. Now they wanted to stop him. But Saul didn't listen to them. He kept teaching and preaching about Jesus.

After a while, some of Saul's Jewish enemies made a plan to get rid of him. Their plan was to watch for him day and night until they caught him. But some of

I learned that . . .

Friends are important! Saul's friends saved his life. They helped him get away from the people who wanted to hurt him.

Saul's friends heard about the plan and told him. They thought of a way to help Saul escape. During the night, they helped Saul get into a big basket. Then they tied a rope to the basket and slowly lowered him over the walls of the city. That's how Saul escaped from those who wanted to hurt him. His friends helped him get away so he would be safe!

I can... Tie a string on a basket or a small box. Put a stuffed animal inside it. Then lower it over the edge of a table or through a staircase railing.

. . . .

Dear God,
Thank you for keeping Saul safe.
Thank you for good friends who help
me and watch out for me. *Amen*

SO I PRAY...

. . . .

**God is our refuge and
strength, always ready to
help in times of trouble.**

PSALM 46:1

Dorcas Is Alive Again

ACTS 9:36-42

There was a woman named Dorcas who lived in the town of Joppa. She was a very kind and generous woman. She was always doing nice things for other people. Dorcas was extra kind and giving to people who were poor. She liked to sew clothing for them.

One day Dorcas got sick, and before long she died. Her friends were very sad. They got her body ready to be buried and put her in an upstairs room. Then they heard that Peter was in a nearby town, so they asked him to come. They knew that God had helped Peter do some amazing miracles.

When Peter arrived, Dorcas's friends took him to the room where her

I learned that . . .

God wants us to be kind and generous, like Dorcas was. She liked to help people and share her time and talents with others.

body was. Women were crowded in the room crying. They missed their friend Dorcas. They showed Peter the coats and clothes that Dorcas had made for them.

Peter asked everyone to leave the room. Then he knelt down by Dorcas's body and prayed. "Get up, Dorcas," he said. She opened her eyes! Peter helped her up and took her out to her friends. Lots of people heard about this and believed in God.

I can... Be generous with others, like Dorcas was. There are lots of ways you can give. Can you share your toys? Can you give someone a present? Can you call someone on the phone who might be lonely?

Dear God,
I want to be kind and generous like Dorcas was. Help me see ways I can help others. *Amen*

Tell [people who are rich] to use their money to do good. They should be rich in good works and generous to those in need, always being ready to share with others.

1 TIMOTHY 6:18

Peter Escapes from Jail

ACTS 12:1-17

King Herod Agrippa was a bad king. He liked to hurt Christians. When he saw that the people liked it when he hurt Christians, he put Peter in jail. Peter was guarded by lots of soldiers. The king was going to put Peter on trial after the Passover. While Peter was in prison, his friends at church prayed very hard for him.

The night before Peter's trial, he was sleeping, chained to two soldiers. Other soldiers stood guard at the prison gate. Suddenly there was a bright light in Peter's cell, and an angel woke him up. "Quick! Get up!" the angel said. Peter's chains fell off his wrists. "Get dressed," the angel said. "Now follow me." The angel led Peter past all of the guards. None of them could see him. Peter walked

I learned that . . .

God protected Peter by sending the angel to help him get out of prison. God answered the prayers of Peter's friends!

right out of prison! When they got outside, the angel disappeared.

Peter hurried to the house where he knew his friends were praying for him. He knocked on the door. The servant girl heard him and knew it was Peter's voice. She was so excited that Peter was there, she forgot to open the door! Finally they opened the door and let him in. He told them about how God had led him out of prison.

I can... Gather three or more people together. Stand alone on one side of a closed door and talk to someone on the other side. Can you tell which person it is?

. . . .

Dear God,
Thank you for protecting Peter and sending an angel to help him. Thank you for answering the prayers of Peter's friends. *Amen*

SO I PRAY...

. . . .

Build each other up in your most holy faith, pray in the power of the Holy Spirit, and await the mercy of our Lord Jesus Christ.

JUDE 1:20-21

Singing in Jail

ACTS 16:16-34

One day Paul and Silas saw a girl who had a bad spirit inside her. Some men used her to make money by having her tell fortunes. The girl followed Paul and Silas around and shouted that they served Jesus. Finally Paul said, "In the name of Jesus Christ, come out of her!" The bad spirit left, and the girl was all better!

But instead of being happy, people got angry. Since the girl was healed, the men couldn't make money from her anymore. So they got Paul and Silas put into jail. To make sure they didn't escape, the jailer put them in the very center of the jail and put chains on their feet.

Around midnight, Paul and Silas were praying and singing hymns. The other prisoners were

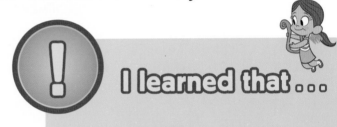

I learned that . . .

Paul and Silas were singing and praising God even when they were in prison! We can thank God no matter where we are and no matter what is happening.

listening to them. Suddenly there was a big earthquake. The walls shook, and the prison doors opened. Every prisoner's chains fell off! The jailer saw that the prison doors were open. He knew he would be in big trouble if the prisoners escaped. But Paul shouted, "It's okay! We're all here!"

The jailer was amazed. So he asked Paul and Silas how he could know Jesus too. They said, "Believe in the Lord Jesus and you will be saved." So the jailer and his whole family became Christians that night.

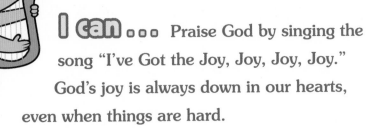

I can... Praise God by singing the song "I've Got the Joy, Joy, Joy, Joy." God's joy is always down in our hearts, even when things are hard.

Dear God,
Thank you for Paul and Silas singing to you while they were in jail. Help me to always praise you no matter what! *Amen*

I will keep on hoping for your help; I will praise you more and more.

PSALM 71:14

The Plan to Get Rid of Paul

ACTS 23:12-35

Paul was in prison, but he didn't do anything wrong. All he did was preach about Jesus. But his enemies said he turned people away from their Jewish teachings.

Paul's enemies wanted to get rid of him. So they got together and made a promise to each other. None of them would eat or drink anything until they got rid of Paul. More than

40 men made this promise.
Then they made a plan to trap Paul. They
would ask for Paul to be brought to a meeting.
But on his way there, they would catch him!

But a young
man heard
about their plan.
He was Paul's
nephew! So he
went to Paul
and told him.
Paul sent his
nephew to a lead
Roman soldier
to explain the
wicked plan.
The lead soldier

I learned that . . .

God can use anyone—
young or old! Paul
was saved from his
enemies because of
a young man.

got a big group of soldiers to go with Paul. There were 200 soldiers, 200 men with spears, and 70 men on horses!

That night the big group of soldiers took Paul to the town of Caesarea. No one could hurt Paul because there were so many soldiers with him! God kept Paul safe from his enemies.

I can... Practice addition. Paul was protected by 200 soldiers, 200 men with spears, and 70 men on horses. Can you add 200 plus 200? Just add 2 plus 2, and then put 2 zeros on the end. Can you add 70 to that? That's how many soldiers went with Paul!

. . . .

Dear God,
Thank you for protecting Paul by using his young nephew. I'm glad that you use young people, not just grown-ups. Please use me, too! *Amen*

SO I PRAY...

. . . .

Don't let anyone think less of you because you are young. Be an example to all believers in what you say, in the way you live, in your love, your faith, and your purity.

1 TIMOTHY 4:12

Jesus Will Come Back

BOOK OF REVELATION

John was sent to the island of Patmos. While he was there, God gave him special messages about the future. He told John a lot about the things that were going to happen many, many years later.

God told John that, one day, all people will be judged. Some of the judgment will be terrible. But God's people will be safe. Then they will go to heaven to live

with Jesus forever.
But people who never believed
in Jesus will not be allowed to enter God's heaven.

John wrote all about the big battle that will
happen someday
between good
and evil—Jesus
and Satan. Jesus
is stronger, so
he will win! Then
Satan will be
thrown into the
lake of fire where
he can never
hurt people
again.

John also
wrote about

I learned that . . .

The promise of
heaven is real!
Jesus will come
back and take all
his followers to
heaven. It will be
a wonderful,
perfect place!

heaven. It is a beautiful and perfect place. Heaven is where everyone who loves Jesus will live with him forever. In heaven, there will be no more death or sadness or crying or pain. God will get rid of all those things! Heaven is for everyone who asks Jesus to live in their hearts and be their Savior.

Someday Jesus will come back and take all his followers to be with him in heaven. John's writing ends with this prayer: "Come, Lord Jesus!"

I can . . . Draw a picture of what you think heaven will look like. Use lots of colors, and make it beautiful!

Dear God,
Thank you for the promise of being in heaven with you someday! I can't wait! *Amen*

SO I PRAY...

He who is the faithful witness to all these things says, "Yes, I am coming soon!" Amen! Come, Lord Jesus!

REVELATION 22:20

Special Bible Verses to Remember

In the beginning God created the heavens and the earth.
Genesis 1:1

I am with you, and I will protect you wherever you go.
Genesis 28:15

The heavens proclaim the glory of God.
Psalm 19:1

The LORD is my shepherd; I have all that I need.
Psalm 23:1

This is the day the LORD has made.
We will rejoice and be glad in it.
Psalm 118:24

Our help is from the LORD, who made heaven and earth.
Psalm 124:8

Thank you for making me so wonderfully complex!
Psalm 139:14

Every word of God proves true.
He is a shield to all who come to him for protection.
Proverbs 30:5

I will strengthen you and keep you.
Isaiah 41:10

Do not be afraid, for I am with you.
Isaiah 43:5

Love your neighbor as yourself.
Matthew 22:39

God loved the world so much that he gave his one
and only Son, so that everyone who believes
in him will not perish but have eternal life.
John 3:16

Whatever you do, do it all for the glory of God.
1 Corinthians 10:31

For I can do everything through Christ,
who gives me strength.
Philippians 4:13

The 10 Commandments

EXODUS 20:2-17

1. Do not worship any other god . . . only the one true God.

2. Do not make anything to honor or pray to. Only honor and pray to God.

3. Do not use God's name in a bad way.

4. Always remember God's special day each week.

5. Love your father and mother and show them respect.

6. Do not kill anyone.

7. If you get married, be a good husband or wife.

8. Do not steal or take things that are not yours.

9. Do not lie about others.

10. Do not want what belongs to someone else.

Facts about Angels

- Angels are God's messengers.

- God gives angels their power. Even the strongest angels stand in awe of God. *Psalm 89:7*

- Angels are mentioned over 250 times in the Bible.

- Moses was amazed as an angel appeared to him in the burning bush. *Exodus 3:2*

- Balaam's talking donkey saw the angel even before he did! *Numbers 22:25*

- God sent an angel to rescue Shadrach, Meshach, and Abednego from the flaming fire. *Daniel 3:28*

- An angel of the Lord came to Joseph in a dream and commanded him to take Mary as his wife. *Matthew 1:20-24*

- The angel Gabriel appeared to Mary with a message from God. Gabriel said, "Don't be afraid, Mary, for you have found favor with God!" Gabriel told Mary that she would give birth to a son, and his name would be Jesus. *Luke 1:26-31*

- Michael is one of the mightiest angels. *Jude 1:9*

- When someone repents and decides to follow God, angels rejoice in heaven. *Luke 15:10*

- We should be kind to everyone. You never know when you might be talking with an angel! *Hebrews 13:2*

- Angels have one main job, and that is to serve God. *Psalm 103:20-21*

- Angels keep God's people out of danger. *Psalm 91:11*

The Miracles of Jesus

Jesus performed many miracles.
These are just a few of them.

- Jesus calmed the storm. *Matthew 8:23-27*

- Jesus walked on the water. *Matthew 14:22-33*

- Jesus healed a blind man. *Mark 10:46-52*

- Jesus healed a man who couldn't walk.
  Luke 5:18-26

- Jesus brought Jairus's daughter back to life.
  Luke 8:40-55

- Jesus healed the lepers. *Luke 17:11-19*

- Jesus turned water into wine. *John 2:1-11*

- Jesus fed a crowd of more than five thousand people. *John 6:1-13*

- Jesus brought Lazarus back to life. *John 11:17-44*

Meet the
Authors & Illustrator

Carolyn Larsen has written more than 40 books for children and adults. She is best known as the author of the Little Girls Bible Storybook line of products, which have collectively sold more than one million units. Carolyn is the mother of three and lives with her husband in Glen Ellyn, Illinois.

Rick Incrocci has over 35 years of experience in graphic arts creating illustrations for children. He specializes in Bible storybooks. Rick has three grown sons and lives with his wife in Lombard, Illinois.

Roma Downey is the President of LightWorkers Media, a production company dedicated to creating positive, uplifting, and inspirational entertainment. LightWorkers' first animated project, Little Angels, is available wherever DVD and digital downloads are sold. Roma was the star of television's *Touched by an Angel* and now serves as spokesperson for Operation Smile, an international children's medical charity that heals children's smiles, forever changing their lives. Roma is married to reality TV pioneer Mark Burnett, and they have three children. Together they are producing a docudrama, *The Bible*, for the History Channel.

May the grace of the Lord Jesus be with God's holy people.

REVELATION 22:21